INdivisible

INdivisible

RADICALLY RETHINKING INCLUSION FOR
SUSTAINABLE BUSINESS RESULTS

Alison Maitland and Rebekah Steele

Young & Joseph Press

Canada • UK

First published in 2020 by
Young & Joseph Press
Canada and UK

For permission requests, contact the publisher at:
www.indivisible-book.com

Names: Maitland, Alison and Steele, Rebekah (authors)
Title: INdivisible: Radically rethinking inclusion for sustainable business results
ISBN: 978-1-7770972-0-2

Subjects: Management I Organizational Development
Typeset in Baskerville and Avenir

Illustrations by J. Rodes Gardner

To my beloved family – AM

To Jenny - big sisters don't have to include little sisters. But you always did. Always. And to Lisa - it is my great joy to interrogate inclusion, to include, and to be included alongside you. – RS

Contents

Case studies

Acknowledgments

We wrote this book in a virtual collaboration spanning the 3,500 miles (nearly 6,000 kilometres) between the UK where Alison lives and Rebekah's home of Canada.

So it seems only right to begin by acknowledging each other. We first met in 2008 and greatly enjoyed exchanging ideas while working together on diversity and inclusion. We found distance surprisingly little obstacle to developing the theme and messages we put forward here.

That is in large part thanks to each other's openness, creativity, listening, generosity and compassion – and our shared eagerness to find more effective ways to advance inclusion in organizations and society.

The technology, which mostly served us well, had the occasional 'off' day when it took patience to persist through pixelated vision and distorted sound. It was a joy when we were able to spend a week together in Ontario putting finishing touches to our draft manuscript.

We have benefited hugely from seeking the advice and perspectives of other people, particularly from Janine Duchar's astute and uplifting guidance and support, David Learmond's generously shared wisdom and experience, and the refinements suggested by the renowned inclusion and diversity experts May Snowden and Nadia Younes. A special thanks to Lisa Wenger for her sage insights, research skills, and abundant contributions working alongside us in producing this book from the start to the finish.

We are grateful to all those who agreed to share their experiences for the case studies we gathered from different sectors and countries. The enthusiastic responses we received from our endorsers on the back cover have made the long months of writing feel even more worthwhile. Thank you so much!

We appreciate all the people with whom we have had fruitful conversations on this topic over the years, including Sanja Haas, who regularly joined our early discussions that eventually led to this book.

We admire the creativity, diligence and artistic integrity of Rodes Gardner. His stunning illustrations beautifully enhance this book.

Then there are the people who have always been there for us during the all-consuming process of developing our ideas and writing the book: David and Lisa. For their constant love and support, words will never be enough. Thank you.

We have sought to be inclusive in the design and approach we have taken with the book. If you find shortcomings in what we have written, let us know so we can learn and improve.

Alison and Rebekah
February 2020

"I have Asperger's and that means I'm sometimes a bit different from the norm. And – given the right circumstances – being different is a superpower."

Greta Thunberg, climate activist

INTRODUCTION

Creating Inclusion with Impact

Harnessing our collective superpower

THIS BOOK is for people who want to build more human, purposeful and sustainable organizations.

When inclusion flourishes, it permeates the whole work environment. It enables everyone to succeed, and it leaves no one out. It has a positive impact on people's desire to work for an organization and how productive they are, the quality of decision-making, customer relations, innovation, revenues and reputation.

Inclusion does not live in a silo. It is indivisible from the way the whole organization operates.

Advancing inclusion is essential for organizations to achieve their goals and be successful over the long term. So this book is for CEOs intent on aligning profit with purpose. It is for finance officers and investors eager to understand the impact of inclusion on the bottom line. It is for risk officers working to avoid the fallout of bias and discrimination. It is for innovation leaders looking for unconventional ideas.

It is for those who devise, implement and oversee Diversity and Inclusion (D&I) strategies, whether as board directors, lead executives, senior sponsors or steering committee members. The fresh perspectives and evidence we provide will give you the reference points and the vision you need to make a world of difference.

This book is also aimed at middle managers and individual contributors. Inclusion benefits everyone, and everyone has a role to play in advancing it.

There are insights for everyone and every function.

Many organizations look to human resources and communications to lead their inclusion efforts. We go beyond this to address functions from research and design through operations to marketing and sales. We take into account external relations with suppliers, investors and governments. There is also crucial learning for students of business, leadership and organizational design.

Whatever your role at your organization, we invite you to dive in.

What you will learn

This book is *not* going to tell you there are a handful of simple changes you can make to find out how people really feel, to raise awareness, or to ensure your leaders behave inclusively. Nor will it tell you that, by doing these things, you will 'solve inclusion' and be able to move on.

This book *is* going to tell you what impact is possible for you, your organization and society if you abandon piecemeal approaches and adopt a bold, ambitious and comprehensive inclusion strategy.

Inclusion today is an overused but under-delivered promise. To achieve powerful and lasting results, organizations need to know exactly WHY it matters to them, HOW to evaluate its impact, and WHAT actions to take for maximum effect – just as you would for any other business strategy.

Using a step-by-step approach, with plenty of practical examples, we explain the WHY, HOW and WHAT.

We offer advice and propose actions for senior leaders who shape company strategy and structures and set the tone for organizational behavior and results.

We share practical measures for middle managers who are at the sharp end of implementing strategy, and who influence employees' day to day working lives. Being skilled at inclusion is crucial for them to succeed in the fast-changing world of work.

We provide learning and actions for individuals because each of us has an effect on the whole system, whether we choose to engage or to stand on the side-lines.

Inclusion is about achieving sustainable positive results by creating environments in which every person matters and the value of every person is inextricably linked to the success of the whole organization. It is about harnessing our collective superpower. If you are excited by that vision, this book is for you – the leader with the formal title, and the leader inside each individual.

CHAPTER 1

Missed Opportunities

Chapter 1 Sections
The gap between words and results
Why focus specifically on inclusion?
- Performance
- Preparedness
- Purpose

Piecemeal approaches
Inclusion with IMPACT

The gap between words and results

EVERYWHERE WE LOOK in the world there is disruption, driving waves of change through business and society. Some of it is positive. Some is deeply divisive.

No organization, leader or individual can hope to survive or manage alone in this swirling sea of change. Connection, collaboration and co-creation are essential. Organizations need to draw on everyone's strengths and perspectives to find answers to the huge challenges ahead. To do that, we must get inclusion right.

Most organizations *want* to be better at inclusion. Over 70% of companies say they aspire to have an inclusive culture.[1]

Business leaders increasingly see this as their responsibility. In the US, more than 700 CEOs and Presidents have signed the CEO Action for Diversity & Inclusion™ Pledge for more inclusive workplaces. The Chairs and CEOs of over 50 large European companies have made a similar pledge (#EmbraceDifference).

These are positive developments.

However, pledges and aspirations are not yet translating into the results leaders say they want. Progress in creating inclusive work environments remains elusive, as the following points demonstrate:

- A broad range of talent continues to be excluded from senior roles.
- Gender, race, disability and other pay gaps remain significant.
- There is a continuing need for campaigns against harassment and discrimination, such as #MeToo and It Gets Better.
- Over 60% of people at work hide or downplay part of who they are to try to fit in with the mainstream, often leaving them isolated and debilitated.[2]
- We have encountered concern in organizations about employees being distressed and distracted, and about lost productivity, because of traumatic events in society that target groups of people for their perceived difference.

- HR executives say they are seriously concerned by the lack of an inclusive innovation culture that invites ideas and encourages collaboration among different people.[3]
- Even the most committed companies are still uncertain how to understand and measure inclusion.[4] In our experience, many define it very narrowly, confuse it with diversity, or have difficulty connecting it with business outcomes.

We know that the lack of progress is causing growing frustration inside companies. Leaders are searching for more effective approaches.

The head of D&I at a multinational company confided to us: "Despite our focus on inclusive leadership, we're still struggling with (achieving) an inclusive culture. What haven't we done right?"

This leader is not alone in seeking a better way forward.

Why focus specifically on inclusion?

Inclusion and diversity are closely linked, but they are not the same thing.

Diversity – the vast mix of individuals, identities, talents, experiences and perspectives in the world and the workforce – is a reality. Diversity is often seen as a problem that organizations need to fix. It is actually an opportunity for organizations to seize.

Inclusion is seizing that opportunity. It unleashes the power of everyone – our collective superpower.

Without inclusion, diversity is unfulfilled potential. We explore this distinction further in Chapter 2.

Diversity, along with inclusion, has been a major element of the authors' professional lives for more than two decades. Our decision to focus on inclusion does not mean that we believe diversity is 'done'. We often hear leaders anticipating that inclusion alone will enable diversity to flourish without further effort, but that's a flawed assumption.

Diversity strategies that address systemic barriers in society and in workplaces remain indispensable. Legislation and the blunt instrument of quotas have proven to be effective in disrupting the status quo. In some cases, they have created a 'new normal' in terms of representation – as the gender-balanced corporate boards in France and Norway demonstrate. Public diversity rankings have also forced change by shining a spotlight on the most successful and the most resistant companies.

But these methods do not guarantee sustained results, and they can unintentionally fuel resentment and backlash. Meanwhile voluntary diversity initiatives, which are less contentious, struggle to make headway, as we explore in Chapter 2.

Our search for breakthrough approaches to Diversity and Inclusion led us to see that inclusion is often the poor relation of diversity. We have heard hundreds of D&I leaders asking what inclusion really is, what strategies and actions increase it, and how to measure it and the impact it has on the business. We realized that if organizations could find answers to these questions, and elevate inclusion to its rightful importance, they could finally achieve the results they are seeking.

There are three overarching reasons why it's critical to get inclusion right: performance, preparedness, and purpose.

Performance

Many companies pay lip service to inclusion. But few are yet able to make a compelling case for harnessing its power to drive their own business performance. This is not for lack of evidence.

Here are some examples of the wide-ranging business impacts of inclusion:

Enhanced team performance: When an individual is excluded within a group, their problem-solving skills tend to diminish, a dynamic that can impact broader team performance.[5] But in inclusive teams, everyone is able to contribute, and people are better positioned to pay attention to each other's views. Research shows that inclusive teams outperform those with lower 'social intelligence'.[6]

Consistent innovation: Companies with a track record of continual innovation are far more likely to describe themselves as 'highly inclusive' than those that innovate only sporadically, a study by The Conference Board found.[7] Rebekah, with management consultant Marjorie Derven, found that the most innovative businesses are better at a whole range of inclusive activities: promoting idea-sharing, encouraging input from a wide range of external collaborators; communicating the strategic importance of inclusion; and holding employees accountable for helping to create the right kind of work environment.[8]

Productive diversity: Diverse teams have the potential to be smarter and more innovative than teams in which everyone is similar. In the absence of inclusive practices, however, they also tend to experience higher rates of friction and turnover. Managers who develop high-quality relationships with all members of the team can significantly cut employee churn by reducing misunderstandings and unhealthy conflicts.[9] This saves money on hiring and helps diverse teams achieve their potential to outperform.

Smarter decision-making: The dangers of 'groupthink' – when conforming leads to poor decisions – have been highlighted in recent years. Transparent, inclusive systems designed to increase diversity in decision-making can reduce this risk and boost productivity, innovation, market knowledge and revenues. In a revealing paper, Cloverpop, a San Francisco-based provider of an enterprise decision platform, describes how it discovered flaws in its own decision-making (it was unintentionally excluding women). It rectified these flaws, with dramatic business results.[10]

Increased loyalty: Young people feel greater loyalty to companies that encourage open communication, ideas from all employees, and mutual support and tolerance, according to research by Deloitte.[11] These are all hallmarks of an inclusive work environment.

Improved wellbeing: Evidence from neuroimaging shows that the same area of the brain activates when people feel physical pain as when they feel the emotional pain of exclusion.[12] Research also shows that people who behave inclusively towards others can gain physical health benefits, such as decreased risk of cardiovascular disease.[13]

So, designing and implementing a comprehensive inclusion strategy can help your organization to:

- Improve collaboration and team performance
- Drive innovation and growth

- Raise productivity
- Save money
- Reduce risk
- Make better decisions
- Increase employee motivation, loyalty and accountability
- Promote employee health and wellbeing
- Enhance relationships with customers and other stakeholders
- Boost revenues

There are case studies throughout the book illustrating many of these business opportunities.

Preparedness

The technological revolution, with its huge opportunities and risks, brings new incentives to invest in designing environments that work for everyone.

Here are key reasons why focusing on inclusion can help organizations adapt and prepare for the challenges of digital transformation:

Transparency: The ease of online communication and messaging through social media has enabled campaigns such as #MeToo and #TimesUp to challenge harassment and other excluding behavior on a previously unimagined scale. Investors, regulators, customers and employees are ratcheting up the pressure on companies to report what they are doing to counter discrimination and promote inclusion. Nearly 70% of employees say that pay transparency is important, and websites such as Glassdoor make it easy to compare salaries.[14] Fine words with little action do not stand up in this era of heightened scrutiny. Companies can only withstand transparency if they have a genuine story to tell, backed up by evidence.

Skills: In a world of smart machines, people must develop not only technological skills but also strong interpersonal skills, such as social influence, flexibility and emotional intelligence. Organizational structures are also changing, with greater emphasis on self-management, collective intelligence and leadership, authentic expression and co-creation. As Frederic Laloux writes in his influential book, *Reinventing Organizations*, "This next stage [of human consciousness] involves taming our ego and searching for more authentic, more wholesome ways of being."[15] Inclusive behavior is all about higher-level human skills and investing in inclusion is a powerful way to equip your workforce for the new world of work.

The fluid workforce: Workers with in-demand skills have vast choice about how and where they work, so companies need tailored approaches to attract and motivate this diverse and mobile workforce. A comprehensive inclusion strategy respects each person's whole identity and individual work style. It also extends to the 'on demand' workforce on whose services companies increasingly rely – from well-paid consultants through to couriers and cleaners – and builds trust, loyalty and a sense of community.

Impact of artificial intelligence: AI brings risks as well as opportunities. Without deliberate planning and intervention, it can replicate and reinforce exclusion. Numerous cases have highlighted race or gender discrimination in AI systems. However, when designed by diverse teams, with inclusion front of mind, AI can be used to detect bias and to help eliminate discrimination in areas like recruitment, or access to training.

Purpose

Alongside rising activism over the climate emergency, discrimination and inequality, the capitalist system itself is under challenge. At the start of 2020, the widely watched Edelman Trust Barometer reported the stark finding that 56% of respondents globally believe capitalism in its current form is doing more harm than good.[16] Negative mentions of business in the media have risen 24% over the past five years, says reputation research firm Echo Research.[17]

The rise of the sharing economy (also known as the peer-to-peer, or 'on demand' economy) reflects a shift towards access rather than ownership. Platforms for ride sharing, workspace sharing, idea sharing, and job sharing help large numbers of people to connect with each other to share assets at low cost to companies and consumers. This new economy is projected to keep growing significantly over the next few years.[18]

Such developments are driving businesses to set out their purpose beyond profits. A few have been doing this for years, but others are now joining in. The US Business Roundtable, an influential group with nearly 200 members, issued a statement in 2019 'redefining' the purpose of corporations. It said companies should protect the environment, foster diversity, inclusion, respect and dignity at work, and support communities, all while generating long-term value for shareholders.[19]

Government interventions are critical, but companies can also play an important role in bridging divides and fostering inclusion, both inside and beyond their boundaries. There is a strong case for them to do so, as this is a way to increase reputation, talent attraction, and brand loyalty. Deloitte's Millennial Survey, for example, found that young workers are looking for employers with a strong sense of purpose beyond financial success.[20]

Responsible companies are aware they must work hard to win and keep their 'social licence to operate'. One way to do this is to use their voice to advance inclusion in society, just as progressive businesses are promoting environmental sustainability across their operations.

The common ground between inclusion and sustainability is now attracting attention as a way to give greater meaning and purpose to work, providing motivation for employees and building trust with stakeholders such as customers, investors, and communities.[21]

Preserving our planet and tackling climate change is the biggest challenge humans have faced. Inclusion plays an important part in addressing this. The climate emergency requires international and local responses that draw on the collective intelligence of many different people, including those most directly affected. Involving a wide range of perspectives and ideas can generate better solutions while ensuring a safe and sustainable environment for even the most vulnerable populations.

There's more on this in Chapters 7 and 10.

To sum up: performance, preparedness, purpose

To stay relevant and competitive, companies must respond and adapt to these multiple forces changing our world and workplaces.

Organizations cannot find breakthrough business solutions by relying on just a few leaders at the top. They must draw on the collective intelligence and commitment of the broadest possible mix of people.

Creating environments where everyone has the resources, support and encouragement to contribute is more important than ever.

With smart action, we can also use inclusion to help us address the broader business, social, and environmental challenges ahead.

> Inclusion is not just a good thing to do. Inclusion is indivisible from the success and sustainability of organizations.

Piecemeal approaches

With all this evidence about why inclusion matters to business results, you might question why progress is so slow.

Why are so many companies stuck? In our experience, it's because they take a piecemeal approach to inclusion. We see businesses around the world falling into some common traps. For example, does your company:

- Fail to connect inclusion with business goals?
- Treat inclusion as an afterthought, following 'diversity and ...'?
- Say 'inclusion' when actually talking about diversity numbers?
- Try to assess inclusion with a few general questions in an engagement survey?

- Measure how people feel but not how they act or what organizational factors are involved?
- Train only senior leaders in inclusive behavior?
- Target inclusion efforts only at 'top talent'?
- Lack a communication strategy highlighting inclusive behavior, actions and results?
- Overlook inclusion in external relationships?
- Replicate 'best practices' from other companies, even when there is evidence they are ineffective?

These traps mean that it is difficult for leaders to see a clear link between inclusion and their strategic goals, so they have difficulty measuring progress and results in a meaningful way.

In the absence of clear understanding and measurement, leaders struggle to answer these critical questions:

1. How inclusive are we today?
2. What progress are we making?
3. What is leading to best results?
4. What gives us the best return on investment?
5. What should we stop doing?
6. How widespread and sustainable are the results we're seeing?
7. How is inclusion supporting our relationships with external partners?
8. How is it helping us achieve our purpose and goals?

Without shared understanding at all levels and robust metrics, progress is difficult to achieve. Decisions are made without data to support them. The opportunities presented by a fully inclusive work environment are missed. The damage caused by exclusion continues.

Inclusion with IMPACT

If you want different results, you have to take a different approach. In fact, you have to take a *whole new* approach.

In this book, we explain the limitations of current initiatives and set out our comprehensive approach to help you to:

Understand inclusion in tangible ways: What is it all about? What needs to be in place? How does it deliver more powerful business results? How does it impact everyday life inside and outside your organization?

Measure these impacts more effectively: How inclusive is your organization currently? What difference does inclusion make? What's missing in your current strategy? How could you do better?

Act to build a more inclusive work environment: What behavior makes a difference at every level of the organization? How can you extend inclusion to your external stakeholders? How can you learn from, and positively impact, inclusion in society?

Organizations need to start asking different questions to get better results. Throughout the book, we present questions and actions for senior leaders to help you identify what you need to do to design and implement a comprehensive strategy. We also provide questions and actions for managers and individuals at all levels, so you can gain a deeper understanding of what inclusion is, how it impacts team and organizational performance, and how it can be put in practice.

We show you how to make progress with practical and significant actions every day, while simultaneously building the structures you need for impactful and sustainable change.

We give you plenty of real-life examples and we prompt you to consider your own ideas and reflections.

As with other business imperatives, cultivating inclusion requires consistent effort. Even so, it doesn't have to be overwhelming.

We take it step by step. Each of the following chapters covers a key element of understanding, measuring and taking action on inclusion. Taking all of these steps into account as an indivisible whole will enable you to design an inclusion strategy that delivers more impactful results for your organization, and for society.

Together, these steps add up to our whole new approach, which is called Inclusion IMPACT®. We pull it all together, including the results you can achieve, in Chapters 8 and 9.

Let's get started.

Read on to see how inclusion gets confused with diversity, why that's a problem and what to do about it.

Notes

1   Bourke, J., Garr, S., van Berkel, A., & Wong, J. (2017, March 1). Diversity and inclusion: The reality gap. *Deloitte Insights.* Retrieved from https://www2.deloitte.com/us/en/insights/focus/human-capital-trends/2017/diversity-and-inclusion-at-the-workplace.html

2   Deloitte (2019). *Uncovering Talent: A new model of inclusion.* Retrieved from https://www2.deloitte.com/content/dam/Deloitte/us/Documents/about-deloitte/us-about-deloitte-uncovering-talent-a-new-model-of-inclusion.pdf

3   The Conference Board (2018, August). The Future of Work: Frontline Challenges in an Era of Digital Transformation. *Research Report.* Retrieved from https://www.conference-board.org/publications/Frontline-Challenges-Digital-Transformation-Era

4   The Conference Board (2019, January). Defining and Measuring Inclusion: Using metrics to drive progress. *Research Report.* Retrieved from https://www.conference-board.org/topics/measuring-inclusion

5   Baumeister, R. F., Twenge, J. M., & Nuss, C. K. (2002). Effects of social exclusion on cognitive processes: anticipated aloneness reduces intelligent thought. *Journal of personality and social psychology, 83*(4), 817.

6   Duhigg, C. (2016). What Google learned from its quest to build the perfect team. *The New York Times Magazine, 26,* 2016. And Woolley, A. W., Chabris, C. F., Pentland, A., Hashmi, N., & Malone, T. W. (2010). Evidence for a collective intelligence factor in the performance of human groups. *Science, 330*(6004), 686-688.

7   The Conference Board (2016, January). Inclusion + Innovation: Leveraging Diversity of Thought to Generate Business Growth. *Key Business Issues.* Retrieved from https://www.conference-board.org/topics/inclusion-innovation

8   Steele, R., & Derven, M. (2015). Diversity & Inclusion and innovation: a virtuous cycle. *Industrial and Commercial Training* (47, 1), 1-7. *https://doi.org/10.1108/ICT-09-2014-0063*

[9] Nishii, L. H., & Mayer, D. M. (2010, February). Paving the Path to Performance: Inclusive Leadership Reduces Turnover in Diverse Work Groups. *Cornell Center for Advanced Human Resource Studies Research Link* (3). Retrieved from https://digitalcommons.ilr.cornell.edu/cgi/viewcontent.cgi?article=1004&context=cahrs_researchlink

[10] Larson, E. (n.d.). *White Paper: Hacking Diversity with Inclusive Decision Making.* Retrieved from https://cdn2.hubfs.net/hubfs/2095545/Whitepapers/Cloverpop_Hacking_Diversity_Inclusive_Decision_Making_White_Paper.pdf

[11] Delitte Touche Tohmatsu. (2016). *The 2016 Deloitte Millennial Survey: winning over the next generation of leaders.* Retrieved from https://www2.deloitte.com/content/dam/Deloitte/global/Documents/About-Deloitte/gx-millenial-survey-2016-exec-summary.pdf

[12] Eisenberger, N. I., Lieberman, M. D., & Williams, K. D. (2003). Does rejection hurt? An fMRI study of social exclusion. *Science, 302*(5643), 290-292.

[13] Kok, B. E., Coffey, K. A., Cohn, M. A., Catalino, L. I., Vacharkulksemsuk, T., Algoe, S. B., ... & Fredrickson, B. L. (2013). How positive emotions build physical health: Perceived positive social connections account for the upward spiral between positive emotions and vagal tone. *Psychological science, 24*(7), 1123-1132

[14] Corman, M. (2019, September). Engaging Today's Workforce. Presentation at *The Conference Board D&I Leaders and Employee Engagement and Experience Council Meeting*, Los Angeles, CA.

[15] Laloux, F. (2014). *Reinventing organizations: A guide to creating organizations inspired by the next stage of human consciousness.* Nelson Parker. (see p. 6)

[16] Edelman. (2020). *2020 Edelman Trust Barometer.* Retrieved from https://www.edelman.com/trustbarometer

[17] Echo Research. (2019, September 10). Populism v capitalism – business as a force for good? Retrieved from https://www.echoresearch.com/news-events/populism-vs-capitalism

[18] PWC predicted that five key sharing sectors had the potential to increase global revenues to around $335bn by 2025. See Vaughan, R., & Hawksworth, J. (2014). *The sharing economy: How will it disrupt your business.* PWC. Retrieved from https://pwc.blogs.com/files/sharing-economy-final_0814.pdf

[19] Business Roundtable (2019, August 19) Business Roundtable Redefines the Purpose of a Corporation to Promote 'An Economy That Serves All Americans'. Retrieved from https://www.businessroundtable.org/business-roundtable-redefines-the-purpose-of-a-corporation-to-promote-an-economy-that-serves-all-americans

[20] Delitte Touche Tohmatsu. (2016). *The 2016 Deloitte Millennial Survey: winning over the next generation of leaders.* Retrieved from https://www2.deloitte.com/content/dam/Deloitte/global/Documents/About-Deloitte/gx-millenial-survey-2016-exec-summary.pdf

[21] Anand, R., Sylvan, R. & Lilani, R. (2019). *Common Purpose, The intersection of Diversity & Inclusion and Corporate Responsibility in the United States.* Retrieved from https://us.sodexo.com/files/live/sites/com-us/files/our-impact/CommonPurposePaperFINAL.pdf

CHAPTER 2

More than Diversity &...

Chapter 2 Sections

Inclusion is often mistaken for diversity
- Missing the big picture

Without inclusion, diversity is unfulfilled potential

Overlooking inclusion is risky
- Giant leap for womankind halted in its tracks

Understand: What is inclusion really?
- Losing out on market share

Measure: Like any other business driver

Take action: tools to get started
- Actions for senior leaders, middle managers and individuals

Inclusion is often mistaken for diversity

COMPANIES FREQUENTLY USE the representation of groups as a measure of inclusion. They focus on specific identity groups, such as the ratio of women to men in leadership roles, or the percentage of employees from marginalized racial or ethnic populations in the total workforce.

These are actually indicators of diversity.

While they are a starting point, they tell us only a little about who is in the organization. They do not tell us what is behind the numbers. They do not shed light on people's experiences of inclusion or exclusion. They do not say anything about organizational behavior or structures. They do not show what impact the current numbers are having on business results.

What's more, they reflect only a small part of the whole mix of individuals, identities, talents, experiences and perspectives in an organization. Consider this example:

Missing the big picture

Walmart showcases a wide range of initiatives in its Culture, Diversity & Inclusion Report, and highlights its leaders' commitment to "dialing up our inclusiveness". When it comes to "Diversity & Inclusion by the Numbers", the report states the percentage of women and people of color at different levels in the company and in promotions.

Publishing these numbers is a positive first step: they show there is some way to go before the company's management and officers reflect the employee base.

But the absence of indicators of inclusion in the report makes it hard to understand what is effective and what is not in Walmart's inclusion initiatives, and whether these are feeding through into business results. This is important information for the company and for its employees, customers and investors. Without comprehensive inclusion measures, we cannot see the big picture. We cannot see how the company is seizing the opportunity of diversity.[1]

To understand and advance inclusion, we need to be clear how it is distinctive from diversity.

Inclusion and diversity are
complementary, but different.

Without inclusion, diversity is unfulfilled potential

Evidence abounds of the dynamic contributions diversity can make to businesses' mission, vision, and strategy. For individuals, too, it can enrich lives by adding variety to our experiences, making our differences less isolating and helping us to question assumptions that may block our, or other people's, progress. For societies, it opens up a wider choice of solutions to collective challenges, and cultural diversity can have a positive impact on economic development.[2]

However, there is also ample research showing that many companies pursuing diversity have not reaped the expected benefits, despite much effort:

McKinsey asked 235 European companies in 2012 what they were doing to advance women. It found that 63% of these companies had at least 20 different initiatives in place, and were "investing considerable money and energy". Despite this, "many companies still express their frustration at the absence of more concrete results."[3]

A much-cited 2016 Harvard Business Review article, *Why diversity programs fail*, stated that strategies for controlling bias, which are the basis of most current diversity efforts, had not succeeded in promoting equal opportunities. This includes implicit bias awareness training. "The problem is that we can't motivate people by forcing them to get with the program and punishing them if they don't," wrote Harvard sociology professor Frank Dobbin and Alexandra Kalev of Tel Aviv University. The authors pointed to more effective approaches that involve managers in problem-solving, increase connections within diverse groups, and promote social accountability.[4]

Implicit bias training is a widely used technique in organizations but this practice was shown in another study, published in 2019, to have limited impact on long-term behavior and diversity mix.[5]

Compounding these challenges is the fact that many companies benchmark against their peers' 'best practices', reproducing the same limited tactics instead of seeking effective alternatives.

Dobbin states: "It shouldn't be surprising that most diversity programs aren't increasing diversity. Despite a few new bells and whistles courtesy of big data, companies are basically doubling down on the same approaches they've used since the 1960s – which often makes things worse, not better."

It is not surprising that many Diversity and Inclusion efforts are stuck.

Overlooking inclusion is risky

Organizations that aim for diverse representation but ignore inclusion run into problems. They might make initial progress on attracting a diverse mix of people. Without inclusion, however, the work environment is suboptimal, or worse. This can lead to costly consequences, including:

- Unfair barriers to development, career progression, and rewards
- Lower engagement, retention and performance
- Experiences of isolation and distraction from work due to the effort to 'fit in'
- Blocked creativity

- Poor collaboration and unhealthy conflict
- Backlash from the majority against perceptions of 'special treatment'
- Reputational damage to the company

Here's one example, relating specifically to gender but illustrative of the wider point.

Giant leap for womankind halted in its tracks

Organizations often have good intentions for drawing on all their talent. But these can be stymied by failing to put in place inclusive systems that anticipate a variety of needs.

In March 2019, NASA's much-heralded plan for the first all-female space walk by Christina Koch and Anne McClain came to an abrupt end because a suitable space suit could not be provided in time. Instead, Koch carried out the assignment with male colleague Nick Hague who replaced McClain.

Astronauts can grow taller in the microgravity of space, and NASA said that McClain had learned during her first spacewalk that a medium-size hard upper torso – essentially the shirt of the spacesuit – fitted her best. However, "because only one medium-size torso can be made ready by Friday, March 29, Koch will wear it."

The postponement – and the reasons given – attracted widespread coverage, and criticism. Fortunately, NASA was able to rectify the problem. The historic all-female walk, on this occasion involving Koch and fellow astronaut Jessica Meir, was rescheduled and took place seven months later, in October 2019, this time with the right number of suitable, readied spacesuits. By that time, however, McClain had returned to Earth.[6]

Some question the evidence about
the value of diversity.

But the problem isn't diversity per se.
It's that diversity does not flourish
without the right conditions.

In commercial terms, an organization is better able to get a return on its investment in people when it actively encourages them to offer up distinctive ideas, perspectives, and expertise. As we saw in Chapter 1, that return can include greater productivity, collaboration, innovation and other business results.

Put simply, why would you hire individuals for their distinctive skills and experiences but then prevent them from fully contributing? Why would you run the risk of losing them?

Diversity needs inclusion to fulfil its promise. That means organizations must thoroughly understand what inclusion is, how to cultivate it and how to measure it.

Rohini Anand, respected former head of corporate responsibility and global chief diversity officer of Sodexo, the multinational services company, agrees that new approaches are called for.

"Diversity without inclusion is a promise unfulfilled," she said. "There need to be more sophisticated ways to measure belonging, inclusion and the impact on business outcomes. We need to use different strategies to have an impact, make a difference and make this work more sustainable."[7]

Understand: What is inclusion really?

If you have difficulty defining inclusion clearly, you are not alone.

In our research and experience with companies, we have found that leaders often struggle to define inclusion in tangible, useful ways. They know it matters, but they are not exactly sure why. It feels abstract, fuzzy, and hard to put into words.

This means there is often an incomplete understanding of what it takes to build and sustain environments that work for everyone. Unfamiliar with the enablers required, leaders can fall prey to the attractiveness of simple answers, instead of investing in the work needed to achieve widespread and enduring inclusion.

A helpful way to define why inclusion matters for your organization is to understand the negative impact of *exclusion*. Here is a case in point.

Losing out on market share

A technology start-up company designed an innovative gesture recognition device with widespread applications, and launched it to initial acclaim. This technology enables humans to interact with devices without physically touching them, just using body language.

Only after launch did the company realize its mistake: it had failed to test the product on a wide mix of consumers. The device did not work well for left-handed users, or for people with smaller extremities, typically women. It had left these customers out.

- What if the company had put an inclusive design process in place for all new products?
- What if the designers had sought out a wider range of perspectives at the start to help them consider all potential users?
- What if they had developed and tried out a prototype with a broad array of consumers?

They could have had a larger market share and greater business success.

Inclusive design and product development could have strengthened their brand reputation.

Instead, they further disappointed market segments that are often under-served by technological breakthroughs.

This company learned the value of inclusion the hard way, by discovering that exclusion damaged its competitiveness. Taking advantage of the lessons from this setback, it updated its business strategy and integrated inclusion into its development of new products.

Overlooking important market segments is just one of the business risks companies run when they have an insufficient understanding of why inclusion matters.

They may fail to take action on structural biases that are, unintentionally but systematically, disenfranchising some employees, causing high rates of turnover and reducing innovation. They may lose the trust of employees, who see a yawning gap between the rhetoric of 'valuing and respecting all our people' and the reality. Consequently, their investment in diversity and inclusion initiatives may yield a poor return.

Measure: Like any other business driver

As inclusion contributes to performance, companies need to measure it in the same way as they measure other business drivers.

Here are some new ways to think about measuring inclusion, comparing it to finance, marketing, safety, and strategic workforce planning decisions:

Finance departments do not look only at gross income and costs. Analysts take account of myriad complex factors and inter-relationships to gain a deep understanding of the financial health of an organization. They share these internally and with investors. Senior managers define very specific financial targets and plans to achieve them. They need to understand how the company's financial situation is changing, so they measure it monthly and quarterly. They look at trends over time and calculate estimates of where they will be in the future. Why not do the same with inclusion?

Marketing departments do not simply count different consumers without understanding the reasons for their purchasing patterns or how to alter them in the company's favor. They gain insights from numbers and from things that are hard to put numbers to, such as brand reputation. They address human behavior, in all its messiness. They don't say that markets are too complex to measure and therefore give up. They dig into that complexity and do their best. Why not do the same with inclusion?

Safety decisions are not based solely on asking employees if they *feel* safe as part of the annual engagement survey. Companies establish clear targets. They perform thorough safety audits, looking for ways to make the organization safer for everyone. Conscious that humans aren't perfect, they adapt systems and processes so that safety does not depend only upon the individual efforts of those working there at any given time. Why not do the same with inclusion?

Strategic Workforce Planning is not just HR's general estimate of future staffing requirements. Making sure an organization has the right people in place at the right time to execute a business strategy requires various data-driven forecasts based on different scenarios. This has to be integrated with other business planning processes. Why not do the same with inclusion?

In other areas that impact the whole organization and its myriad relationships, leaders make complex decisions by clarifying desired outcomes, determining how to achieve them, designing robust strategies, and capturing and analyzing data that demonstrate the risks and value of available options, before mapping out a plan of action.

Once implemented, they measure the outcomes, impacts and return on investing in that course of action. That informs what they do next. They invest in a whole range of resources that make strategic planning and analysis possible, including expertise, staff, and software. Where strategies and metrics are considered central to operating successfully, organizations invest heavily.

Why settle for less than this with inclusion?

Take action: Tools to get started

With diversity, you probably focus on attracting a mix of people into your organization and striving for more balanced representation throughout. Inclusion requires that you create an environment where that mix of people can be their best.

As we explain over the next chapters, organizations must take a whole-system approach if they want to make serious and sustainable progress with inclusion. That means starting by reviewing your organization's purpose and aspirations and asking: What do we need to achieve these? How can we measure progress along the way? This review needs to be inclusive itself, involving a broad mix of people connected with the organization right at the beginning. In this way, inclusion becomes an indivisible part of your business strategy and operations.

As you embark on this, you can also take some simple steps to make a difference right way. Here are some examples.

Actions for senior leaders, middle managers and individuals

Senior Leaders

- Start to ask this question in every strategy meeting: "Who will share a different idea to help us be more discerning and more creative?"
- Explore with colleagues how you can formalize this as part of every business meeting in your organization.

Middle Managers

- Ask your direct reports what you can do to make it easy for each of them to speak freely and share their ideas and dissenting opinions.
- Use their guidance to adjust how you run meetings.
- Share what you learn with other managers.

Individuals

- Help others on your team to speak up by making opportunities to listen, ask questions, and create a safe space.
- Talk with your co-workers and manager about how to ensure that everyone has a voice, including in how the team operates and how work gets done.

Making time: Taking action means starting new habits. To be successful, you also need to consider what you will *stop* doing. Rather than hoping to find time for inclusion, intentionally structure in time to connect with people, to listen to someone with whom you disagree, to implement the suggestions in this book and to develop the capabilities to do this well.

Meanwhile, put an end to old routines that work against your inclusion efforts. For example, you might stop 'multitasking' on your smartphone in meetings instead of giving all colleagues your full attention. Or stop using idioms and metaphors that are specific to one culture. Or stop assuming that colleagues who rarely speak up in meetings have nothing to say and instead intentionally invite their contribution. Eliminate time-wasting diversions in order to open up the time you need to begin your new steps to build inclusion.

Evaluating: Monitor and evaluate the impact you make with these actions on individual engagement, team performance, and business success. You can do this formally if you're a senior leader or middle manager, or informally if you are an individual contributor.

Read on to find out why inclusion is about more than individual employees' experience – and what the bigger picture tells you.

Notes

1   Walmart (2018). *Your Story is Our Story: Culture, Diversity &* *Inclusion 2018 Report.* Retrieved from https://corporate.walmart.com/media-library/document/2018-culture-diversity-inclusion-report/_proxyDocument?id=00000168-4df5-d71b-ad6b-4ffdbfa90001

2   Ashraf, Q., & Galor, O. (2011). *Cultural diversity, geographical isolation, and the origin of the wealth of nations. NBER Working Paper* (No. w17640). National Bureau of Economic Research. Available from https://www.nber.org/papers/w17640

3   McKinsey & Company (2012, March). Women Matter 2012, Making the Breakthrough. Retrieved from https://www.mckinsey.com/business-functions/organization/our-insights/women-matter

4   Dobbin, F., & Kalev, A. (2016, July-August). Why diversity programs fail. *Harvard Business Review.* Retrieved from https://hbr.org/2016/07/why-diversity-programs-fail

5   Forscher, P. S., Lai, C. K., Axt, J. R., Ebersole, C. R., Herman, M., Devine, P. G., & Nosek, B. A. (2019). A meta-analysis of procedures to change implicit measures. *Journal of personality and social psychology, 117*(3), 522.

6   Various news reports including Strickland, A. (2019, October 16). The first all-female spacewalk is scheduled for this week. CNN. Retrieved from https://edition.cnn.com/2019/10/04/world/nasa-koch-meir-first-all-female-spacewalk-scn-trnd/index.html

7   Interview with author (2019, May).

CHAPTER 3

More than Just Me

Chapter 3 Sections

Inclusion is about my experience

I am also responsible for other people's experience

Understand: Inclusion counts at every level - Senior Leaders, Middle Managers and Teams

- Naturally inclusive leaders
- Showing managers 'what's in it for me'

Measure: Detect inconsistencies

- Making everyone responsible for inclusion

Take action: Get everyone on board

- Actions for senior leaders, middle managers and individuals

Inclusion is about my experience

WE KNOW IMPLICITLY that being included is important to us. We like it when other people accept us for who we are. We appreciate it when they are open to hearing our views, especially if our views are different and they still welcome them.

This makes us feel respected and valued. It creates trust. It gives us choice, and the knowledge that we can influence things that affect us. It removes obstacles to our growth, performance, wellbeing and success.

When it comes to the work environment, there is growing evidence of the cost to individuals and businesses when people have to pretend to be something they are not, for fear of rejection or discrimination.[1]

Being free of such constraints is empowering. It releases energy for productive purposes that would otherwise be expended on maintaining a disguise, or fighting stereotypes. If we are at ease being ourselves at work, we can perform better and contribute to making a difference. In turn, this benefits not only us, but also the organization.

Being free to be authentic and 'bring your whole self to work' does not mean you are *required* to share every part of yourself at work. Not everyone is as open as Credit Suisse Director Pippa/Phil Bunce, whose gender expression at work shifts along the feminine-masculine continuum and who has written about this in the *Financial Times*, saying "it is smart [for organizations] to allow people to be authentic".[2] Inclusion does, however, create an open door for each person to determine what they bring about themselves to work.

'Freedom to be myself' is on the rise as a central concept in building inclusion. Some organizations have sought to measure how inclusive they are by asking individuals about their own personal experience.

'Do you feel valued at work?' and 'Are you able to be the real you?' are typical questions put to employees to try to understand the state of inclusion in the organization, usually as part of an employee engagement survey.

These kinds of questions can provide some helpful insights. However, they are only a small part of a much bigger picture.

I am also responsible for other people's experience

While our personal experience matters, there is much more to inclusion than our own individual benefits. Individuals don't exist in a vacuum. What we think, say and do has an impact on others. Our individual needs and self-expression must take account of others. Part of inclusion is being inclusive, and taking care of other people.

We have a responsibility to lift people up, not put them down. We can all benefit from inclusion, but only if we recognize that we are also responsible for advancing inclusion for everyone.

This means there is a balance to be struck. Giving people freedom to be themselves can never extend to bullying, bigotry or making other people feel small or threatened.

So, inclusion is not just about how *I* feel as an individual, or about what is done to *me*. It is also about what impact my action – or inaction – has on others.

To start to see the bigger picture, organizations need to understand and measure this. They must assess not only how individuals feel, but also how those individuals are behaving towards others.

Inclusion is not just about how *I* feel as an individual, or about what is done to *me*.

It is also about what impact my action – or inaction – has on others.

Understand: Inclusion counts at every level

Because everyone is affected, everyone has a part in creating an inclusive work environment. This means taking into account not only individual employees but also middle managers and senior leaders – indeed, every individual involved with an organization. It is difficult to sustain inclusion if you leave anyone out.

There are myriad relationships and interactions going on at every level across the organization every day. To understand how inclusive your work environment is, you need to know more about the dynamics of those relationships and interactions.

For example, a middle manager may treat some members of their team differently from others. A team may be more open to including some members than others. A department may be seen as welcoming by those working there, yet viewed by other departments as unfriendly. Senior leaders may think they are accessible to people across the organization, but employees may view the top team as an insiders' club.

To build a comprehensive inclusion strategy, you have to understand more than individual employees' experiences. You must explore the roles played by leaders, managers and teams.

Let's look at each in turn.

Senior Leaders

Senior leaders play a huge part in ensuring that their organizations make the most of the rich mix of people in their workforce. They influence how others lead and behave, so their actions are far reaching.

In determining the company strategy, they decide what to prioritize and resource. They are responsible for communicating important initiatives. They influence and approve formal processes. They decide who will be hired at senior and middle levels and they hold them accountable for results.

CEOs and other top leaders can also have an impact beyond their organization. They may influence public policy. They may decide to work with peers to highlight the need for wider action and change, for example on the climate emergency, or on human rights in the supply chain. (There's more on this in Chapter 10.)

What senior leaders do to advance inclusion is therefore critical. Recognizing this, many organizations focus all or most of their inclusion work on this top layer of people, typically aiming to raise their awareness of their implicit biases and alter their default behavior.

Increasingly, companies are adding explicit inclusive leadership competencies into the processes used to select, assess, develop, and reward senior leaders.

One multinational conglomerate, for example, recently created a technology-enabled feedback tool for people to rate their leaders on how inclusive they are. These assessments are added to personnel files to help inform decisions about leaders and their career progression opportunities.

Other companies have gone beyond giving feedback and introduced inclusiveness into pay formulas for top leaders, to increase their incentives and accountability.

Naturally inclusive leaders

Guido Horst was not aware of his talent for inclusion until he went on a program called Collective Leadership. As CEO of Ardanta, a subsidiary of the large Dutch insurance group a.s.r., Horst was used to 'being in charge'. He had experienced many leadership courses, none of which had inspired him.

"They were all about a conquering-the-world approach," he says. "You were supposed to brag about the size of your lease car, how many people you are leading and what your turnover is. None of them touched the essence of who I am in the way that Collective Leadership did."

The program, run by Dutch company PresenceAtWork, uses a distinctive assessment method that revealed Horst's strength as an 'integrator'. This means that he has a facility for creating inclusiveness and harmony and making sure that no one is left out or left behind.

At first, he admits he found this hard to accept. For decades, the preferred leadership style had seemed to value only hard facts and double-digit growth. "I was focused on meeting those expectations, trying hard to be the leader that I felt I should be."

Through the program, which he attended in 2014, he realized the value of not always being out in front but instead encouraging others to assume responsibility, step in and take charge when their strengths are needed – the essence of collective leadership. It is a style that comes more naturally to him and that he finds much more fulfilling.

He has seen many benefits, he told Alison, who has also been through the program. For one thing, it lifts some of the weight off his shoulders while enabling others in the organization to grow faster, easing succession planning. It also produces better results. "Together we can do much more than we usually think we can."

He has also learned to balance business rationale with intuition in decision-making. "I used to operate in an environment where 'business cases' were presented as the holy grail. If the figures added up to a positive result, everything should be ok. Now I dare to challenge these figures in the business case and listen, more than I used to, to what I feel and sense with respect to the decision to be made."

In this book, we give plenty of examples of what leaders and others can do to be more inclusive. One of those things is to recognize inclusiveness as a core leadership trait that is needed in any team. While it can be learned – and we provide many actions for leaders to take in this direction – it is important to value those who are naturally inclusive.

What advice does Horst have for other leaders? "To really flourish personally, and to create the circumstances for your organization to be successful, it is important to acknowledge your natural strengths as a CEO – to value what you're good at, and to know where you need someone else to step in," he replies. "When you are OK with who you are, others feel safe to open up as well. It creates a tremendous amount of trust when people feel they can be authentic in their expression. This is how you build an organization based on unity and inclusion. It is a super strong foundation from which to excel."[3]

Middle Managers

It is common knowledge that people tend to leave or stay in an organization because of their immediate supervisor. So the actions of middle managers are crucial contributors to the state of the overall work environment.

Yet for decades, middle management has been described as 'frozen' or 'sticky' when it comes to advancing inclusion. D&I leaders frequently ask how they can get middle managers 'on board'.

When you think about it, this is a surprising question. Middle managers are expected to deliver results for productivity, profit, safety, talent development, and other important objectives. Why not for the business goal of inclusion? Is it because companies have not made clear to middle managers that achieving results from inclusion is integral to their responsibilities?

Organizations can engage their middle managers by making sure they:

- Understand that inclusion is an explicit priority for the business and for them
- Know how it can benefit them and their teams
- Are clear that they are expected to be inclusive
- Know what to do to meet these expectations
- Have a say in the steps they will take
- Have the skills and capabilities to succeed
- Have sufficient resources
- Are supported by senior leaders and by formal processes

- Are held accountable for results through regular reviews – reinforced with rewards when they are successful, and opportunities for improvement (or sanctions if necessary) when they fall short

If your inclusion strategy does not address the needs of middle managers, they won't be in a position to generate business value from inclusion.

If, on the other hand, you help them succeed and hold them accountable for results, you can unlock a powerful force for inclusion at the heart of your organization.

Showing managers 'what's in it for me'

Sodexo, the international services group, is an example of a company that has shown its middle managers why inclusion is important for them and for business outcomes. Managers are held accountable, using performance scorecards, not only for recruiting, retaining and promoting a mix of people, but also for inclusive behavior and action, says Rohini Anand, former global chief diversity officer.

They have to show they have participated in training, integrated messages about diversity and inclusion into their communications, and hosted or engaged in relevant community events.

Managers have also been encouraged to share Sodexo's internal initiatives with clients, including a major study that found teams managed by a balanced mix of women and men perform better than others on a wide range of outcomes.

"They saw the benefit that all of this brought with their clients and it became a differentiator," Anand told us. "Instead of thinking 'there's nothing in this for me', now they saw it could help them grow the business. When they share what we're doing, for example our annual report, or our training, or the Gender Balance Study, they get drawn into a wider web of influence, their profile is elevated, and they say: 'Our competitors aren't doing this – I can leverage it as a competitive advantage with clients'."[4]

Teams

Team dynamics also play a role in cultivating or undermining inclusion. As teams form, break up and re-form, it's important that every member has a say in defining and sharing in how the team operates. They could, for example:

- Learn each other's working preferences and agree how to take them into account effectively
- Co-create guidelines for a safe and respectful environment where all team members can be themselves
- Agree how to deal with conflict in a constructive way
- Be open to, and actively encourage, a variety of opinions

As we've seen from the evidence in Chapter 1, such steps help teams to make smarter decisions, collaborate across differences and be more innovative.

Measure: Detect inconsistencies

Who should be represented in your metrics? The answer is everyone, because everyone benefits from inclusion and everyone is responsible for making it happen. This means addressing not just individuals but also teams, managers and senior leaders.

At the start of this chapter, we gave examples of two questions that employers currently ask to gauge inclusion. To improve your measurement, start asking questions of a sample of people at all levels that challenge them to think about their own role in fostering inclusion, as well as how others behave towards them.

Here are four questions you could ask people across your organization, to broaden how you are evaluating the work environment:

About You: How often do you take account of other people's perspectives at work?

About Your Team: How often do your co-workers value each other's perspectives?

About Your Manager: How often does your manager use opportunities to seek out different viewpoints?

About Senior Leaders: How often do the top leaders *formally* encourage employees to express a wide range of views?

The first question focuses on individuals' assessment of their own behavior towards others. The other three questions are about other people, starting with immediate colleagues, through to supervisors and then to the leadership of the organization.

When you include these questions as part of a comprehensive assessment of your company, the answers can give you a view of how consistently – or inconsistently – people are behaving across the organization.

Inclusion is not a one-way street, although many companies treat it this way. Actually, inclusion is like a well-functioning traffic roundabout or intersection, where people pay attention to everyone else and take turns to yield to each other or move forward, and where everyone's thoughtful actions have an impact on the success of the whole.

The answers to the questions above can also reveal what is going well, and where there are issues to probe further. For example, if the answers to questions 1-3 (about you, your team and your manager) are mostly 'Often', but the answers to question 4 (about senior leaders) are mostly 'Rarely', this would suggest a disconnect between the way people are acting at grassroots level and the behavior at the top of the organization. It would indicate that senior leaders should do more to encourage employees to share their perspectives. It would also show that those at the top could learn about what works by asking front-line employees and managers.

What questions would you add to find out how consistently inclusion is happening across your organization?

An inclusive work environment is like a well-functioning traffic roundabout or intersection.

People pay attention to each other and take turns to yield or to move forward.

Everyone's thoughtful actions have an impact on the success of the whole.

Making everyone responsible for inclusion

During a strategic dialogue with executives at a tech start-up, Rebekah learned that senior leaders were committed to creating a workplace where everyone was included, everyone benefited from inclusion, and everyone was responsible for inclusion. They knew this would help bring their other company values to life. They cited the evidence that this could boost innovation, which was central to their plan to be winners in their marketplace.

They also knew there was work to do to realize this vision. Internal data about barriers to full inclusion reflected trends faced by many companies, such as:

- A belief that focusing on diversity and inclusion would interfere with merit-based evaluations of people
- A traditional leadership framework with ill-defined concepts such as 'executive presence' instead of what's actually needed for effective leadership
- An unwillingness to challenge clients who indirectly, but unmistakably, indicated a preference for working with heterosexual, white men with no observable disabilities
- A pattern of managers subconsciously singling out women to do extra work (e.g. planning socials), distracting them from assignments that were core to promotion
- A prevailing assumption that people should be free to be themselves without worrying about 'political correctness'

With the strategic goal that everyone would be responsible for inclusion, Rebekah helped the company take the following multi-pronged approach:

Employees participated in action-oriented learning, advancing their commitment to support each other and to speak up on behalf of one another. Insights were translated into individual action plans. Right away, employees began addressing barriers to inclusion, with solutions like this:

- Taking responsibility to create space for all to voice perspectives and ideas during meetings, for example by deliberately asking all team members to share their thoughts and by calling out interruptions
- Disrupting observed instances of exclusion by naming them and then starting constructive dialogues to clarify expectations about inclusive behavior

As middle managers also put action plans into play, they realized they had additional responsibility. Beyond changing their own behavior, they began creating new policies and processes that could support and sustain inclusion, such as:

- Revising job postings to better attract both overlooked and mainstream talent in the qualified labor pool
- Moving from informal decisions about compensation to a standard process to support pay equity

Further supporting everyone's individual actions, senior leaders drafted a comprehensive plan to make it safer, easier and more comfortable for all employees to speak freely, and to speak up for others facing barriers. This included:

- Establishing a new company value and a new performance competency. These clarified expectations to speak up and help others do the same
- Incorporating the new competency into performance management, recognition and reward processes to reinforce speaking up

Within three months, leaders reported a notable increase in employees speaking up every day, particularly to disrupt bias and to create space for quiet or dissenting voices to be heard. Leaders appreciated that these individual initiatives reduced the burden on them and on middle managers to deal with issues arising over barriers at work. They also reported other rapidly realized milestones, such as greater involvement in inclusion initiatives, more teams with a mix of diversity, and instances of increased innovation contributing to faster company growth.

Take action: Get everyone on board

Actions for senior leaders, middle managers and individuals

Senior Leaders

- Collaborate with middle managers to establish clear expectations about their inclusion performance and results.
- Discuss how these will help them achieve their objectives, and improve their relationships with employees and stakeholders.
- Support their success by weaving expectations into talent processes such as performance management, succession and rewards.

Middle Managers

- Start an informal coaching group with a mix of junior and senior colleagues at different levels and in different parts of the organization.

- Focus on feedback, sharing ideas, and encouraging each other to succeed.
- Make time to co-create ways to support each other's commitment to inclusion, and start practicing these every day.

Individuals
- Check in regularly with your colleagues to make sure they feel supported and involved with how things are going in the team, on your joint project, or in the organization generally.
- You can set the example, even if you're not the team leader. Encourage your manager to establish a process enabling this for teams across the organization.

Making time: Remember to open up space to take action by eliminating something you are doing now. Double the benefit by choosing to stop something that gets in the way of inclusion.

Evaluating: Be sure to monitor and evaluate the impact that your actions make on individual engagement, team performance and business success.

Addressing the big picture: By taking action, you can start to increase inclusion right away. Individual action is important but insufficient. In the next chapter, we'll say more about how organizations must address their policies and systems, too.

Read on to find out how to take account of more than just how people feel.

Notes

1   Yoshino, K., & Smith, C. (2013). *Uncovering talent: A new model of inclusion.* Retrieved from https://www2.deloitte.com/content/dam/Deloitte/us/Documents/about-deloitte/us-about-deloitte-uncovering-talent-a-new-model-of-inclusion.pdf

2   Bunce, P. (2015, October 19). Mx matters as much as Lord, Prof, Ms and Mr. *Financial Times.* Retrieved from https://www.ft.com/content/08f4b532-70c8-11e5-9b9e-690fdae72044

3   Interview with author (2019, December). And Maitland, A. (2016). *A New Model for Organizations.* Presence at Work. Retrieved from https://presenceatwork.com/public/img/raw/79.presenceatwork_collective-leadership-case-study-ardanta.pdf

4   Interview with author (2019, May) featuring *Sodexo's Gender Balance Study 2018.* Available from www.sodexo.com/inspired-thinking/research-and-reports/gender-balance-study-2018.html

CHAPTER 4

More than Feelings

Chapter 4 Sections

Inclusion *is* about feelings

MANY ORGANIZATIONS seek to understand how inclusive their culture is by asking employees how they *feel* about it.

Does your company ask questions like these?

- Do you feel a sense of belonging, even when something negative happens?
- Do you feel respected for what makes you unique?
- Do you feel your ideas count?
- Do you feel that you are part of a team?
- Do you feel you are given opportunities to develop?
- Do you feel able to speak freely at work?

Understanding employees' feelings of inclusion is an important part of a comprehensive strategy. These perceptions help you evaluate whether your inclusion efforts are having a positive impact. Top leaders might believe the company is making good progress. But if employees don't *feel* included, something is wrong.

Feelings translate into behavior that impacts results, for better or worse. Workers who feel included are more likely to bring their best ideas to work, for example, which in turn boosts innovation.

People who feel left out, on the other hand, are more likely to disengage or leave. Research also suggests there's a bigger risk that people who feel excluded will create a toxic workplace by undermining others, cheating, or lying. [1]

Inclusion is also about much more

While data about employees' feelings can be useful, they are by no means enough.

First, the data tell you only how people are feeling right now in their part of the organization. They do not give you any information about why.

Second, they offer little, if any, clue to how perceptions about the work environment affect business results.

Third, information about feelings does not shed light on the behavior that may be generating those feelings, or the organizational factors that may be undermining or supporting inclusion.

So, asking employees a few questions about how they feel is of limited use. When relying solely on employee perceptions, companies lack the data to understand where things are going well and where they are not. They don't know why people feel as they do, or what broader dynamics underlie individual experiences. Here's a real-life example of what can get missed.

Systemic bias beneath the surface

Kala* was an early-career employee working in a company with positive public statements about diversity but no clear strategy for ensuring an inclusive work environment.

In her answers to the questions in the company's engagement survey, Kala said that she felt valued at work, part of her team, and respected for her unique contribution. So far so good, it seemed.

However, a lot of information was being missed. The few questions she answered in the engagement survey did not provide the company with any idea of why she felt good about her work environment. So the company did not find out that Kala's team and manager were unusual role models for intentionally inclusive ways of working – behavioral information from which it could learn a lot.

Nor did these questions reveal anything about the risk ahead. Kala's positive early experience was later reversed by a lack of fairness and transparency in the processes used to select people for special assignments, development, and future leadership.

As she and her manager fought to gain pay increases, development opportunities, and promotions to reward her high performance and potential, Kala encountered an almost invisible systemic bias giving preference to leadership characteristics associated with the men who had been most successful in the company over recent decades.

Kala's employer, for all its lip service to diversity, failed to assess whether there were structures in place that undermined or enabled its stated inclusion goal of benefiting from the opportunities of a diverse workforce.

These limitations were confusing and frustrating to Kala. They didn't align with her original feelings of inclusion, with her extraordinary performance reviews or her career aspirations. In the face of these confounding barriers, Kala left the company to join an organization with more inclusive structures that accelerated her career growth and related rewards as she became a successful leader. [2]

*Name changed for anonymity

It is extremely difficult to address gaps like these if your organization cannot clearly see or understand them. To avoid such serious oversights, do not rely only on survey data about feelings.

Understand: Actions and organizational structures

In Chapter 3, we began to explore the importance of personal actions in creating and sustaining an inclusive work environment. To understand inclusion, you cannot stop at how people feel. You need to understand the behavior they are demonstrating and the behavior they are experiencing or observing in others.

Actions

How people behave is an expression of inclusion or exclusion. It's important to know if this matches up with people's feelings and is consistent with the organization's professed values.

For example, your company might have a statement about valuing different viewpoints. But unless people at every level are taking consistent action to ask for, share and use viewpoints, the organization is not living up to that value, nor reaping the full benefits of diverse perspectives.

We should explain that when we talk about actions, we are encompassing both intentional *and* subconscious actions and behavior.

An intentional action to include everyone could be the chair of a meeting proactively asking each person to share their views. An example of subconscious excluding behavior would be the chair giving more speaking time to people at the meeting with the same educational background as them. This behavior may not be intentional but its effect, if replicated across the organization, is to create systemic barriers to people from different educational backgrounds.

Actions can have potent impact. So they must be considered as well as feelings, to know whether the behavior of individuals, teams, managers and senior leaders is contributing to or hampering the company's aspiration to be inclusive.

Organizational structures

Most organizations have not been designed and built with inclusion deliberately in mind. As we saw from Kala's story, they are full of subtle but insistent signals that actually get in the way of inclusion. These signals may take the form of widely held assumptions about 'the way we do things here' or the type of person you have to be to get promoted. An individual might *feel* included without realizing that people like them are unintentionally but systematically excluded from leadership.

Without formal processes designed to reinforce inclusion everywhere, building and sustaining an environment that works for all remains difficult, if not impossible.

It is common for organizations to start trying to build inclusion by raising awareness, then moving to changing behavior, and eventually considering systemic changes further down the road – if they get that far.

With our Inclusion IMPACT® approach, structures are an indivisible part of the change you have to make from the start. When inclusion is deeply rooted, it has the chance to grow and spread, withstand turbulence and release oxygen on which the whole organization can thrive.

Let's compare two leaders. Both believe deeply in the principle of equal pay. Leader 1 works in a company where formal structures have been designed to ensure that decisions on pay are fair. Leader 2 works in a company where there are no such structures, and where the leader has to fight against each instance of inequality. Which of these leaders is more likely to achieve sustainable pay equity?

Formal systems and processes to support inclusion must be wide-ranging. They should address key areas, such as:

Opportunities: e.g. fair and transparent access to jobs, career development and 'hot projects'

Flexibility: e.g. choice about working times and locations

Having a voice: e.g. ensuring safe ways for employees and stakeholders to speak up

Total Rewards: e.g. fair pay and customizable benefits, as well as recognition for those who use inclusion effectively to improve business results

Product development: e.g. eliminating bias in software coding or in new product design

External relations: e.g. promoting inclusion with investors, policy makers and suppliers (Learn more on this in Chapter 7)

Measurements: e.g. to demonstrate the positive impact of inclusion on recruitment, productivity, leadership effectiveness, customer satisfaction, and innovation

Here's another real story that shows why it's so important to understand and assess the explicit and implicit systems and structures in your organization.

Curious case of future leader who 'lacked commitment'

Senior managers agreed that Avery* was a strong performer, regularly meeting or exceeding objectives. At the annual meeting to assess high-performing employees' potential to grow into future leaders, there was no dissent on that point.

One executive, however, noted that Avery lacked commitment and was therefore not 'promotion material'.

Rebekah, who was part of the meeting, was surprised by this assessment. She inquired which performance objectives or leadership competencies Avery had failed to meet. Everyone agreed that this talented employee surpassed requirements for results and behavior, including going 'above and beyond' for customers and influencing others to do the same. In that case, why was there any objection to putting Avery forward?

Rebekah asked for specific evidence of 'low commitment'. The problem, the executive replied, was that Avery left work at 5pm every day. This was unusual in a company where the dominant belief was that advancement required long working hours. However, staying after 5pm was not a real requirement and Avery demonstrated outstanding commitment by consistently exceeding expectations.

The aim of the meeting was to identify talented people who could help the company grow sustainably. Avery was clearly one of these, yet was very nearly left out. Because of hidden individual and systemic bias about what 'commitment' and 'leadership' looked like, the company could have been deprived of top leadership material.

Once identified, the bias could be mitigated swiftly. Avery was immediately included in leadership development plans and promoted later that year.

Learning from this, the company also recognized that inclusion requires more than individual awareness and actions. It refined its people processes to make clear the real requirements of 'commitment' – such as doing what you say you will do to meet company goals – and to eradicate rewards based simply on long hours. Leaders went further, developing a strategy for a flexible environment focused on rewarding results, not working hours.

Avery continues to exceed expectations to drive competitive advantage, still leaves work at 5pm most days and now, as a senior executive, leads an inclusive work environment that helps the business grow.

*Name changed for anonymity

Reviewing organizational factors, such as the HR processes and implicit assumptions in this case, yields a better understanding of how to foster inclusion to support both individuals and business goals.

This is especially important for people who feel they may be stereotyped as 'less able'. A practical way for leaders to overcome this concern is to signal a belief that everyone, not just a select few, has the potential to perform at the highest level.

A lab experiment at a US state university found that overt signaling increased the likelihood that women and minorities would apply for a new science, technology and engineering (STEM) course. "Signaling a belief in potential as widespread can speak to women and minorities' sense of belonging and ... turn down the volume of their concern about being stereotyped," explains Aneeta Rattan, associate professor of organizational behavior at London Business School.

In her experiment, the typical gap between African American and European American students' interest in STEM courses closed, as did the gap between women's and men's interest in the courses.[3]

Pointers and signals like these are an essential part of a comprehensive inclusion strategy. Without them, it is easy to leave people out, even if that is not our conscious intention.

The US psychologist Deborah L Plummer uses the term 'We' to encapsulate inclusion. This is how she puts it: "Getting to We demands a laser-like focus on inclusive policies and strategies. The feeling of inclusion will follow."[4]

Changing the whole system

When it comes to organizational factors, robust inclusion requires more than addressing single factors one at a time. It is common for companies to focus on adjusting one part of their organization, such as leadership behavior, in an attempt to broaden opportunities for all. But, as we've said, piecemeal changes of this kind do not deliver sustainable results.

Just as a seed requires a nurturing ecosystem of fertile soil, water and light to grow, inclusion needs a thriving ecosystem for success. Organizations are comprised of interdependent elements: the business strategy, organizational structure, processes, a leadership strategy that clarifies expectations, workers' capabilities, individual assumptions and behavior, and metrics and rewards. See diagram below.

Ecosystem Approach

Steele and Galusha ecosystem approach to widespread change [5]

For inclusion to thrive, change must be comprehensively woven throughout the ecosystem. Each component must be analyzed and adjusted, as necessary, to ensure that it reinforces the desired change and works in harmony with all others.

For example, if your organization makes a decision to formally recognize inclusion as critical to its business strategy, this commitment must also be reflected in:

- How leaders are selected and held accountable
- Employee beliefs about the organization
- Employee skills
- Roles and structures that support inclusion
- Metrics

In the absence of simultaneous and comprehensive change throughout the ecosystem, old habits and entrenched processes will slow or even prevent your desired impact. For instance, a company decides to introduce an agile working policy and give everyone greater autonomy and choice, to enable a wide variety of working preferences. But it does not alter its rewards process. People continue to be rewarded and promoted based on presence in the office. Initial enthusiasm about the new way of working turns to disillusionment, causing the intended change to backfire.

Measure: Uncover the gaps

Supposing your company has 'inclusion' as a stated value, but your employee engagement survey shows that some people are feeling less included than in your last survey. It looks as though the organization is not living up to its rhetoric. You analyze the data to see which workforce segments are most affected.

What then? Unless you are also assessing how people are behaving and whether you have structures in place to support inclusion, you won't know how to start addressing the problems you've found.

For example, you won't know that your leadership identification process is failing. You won't know that hidden biases are holding people back from promotion. You won't know that you run the risk of losing high performers to the competition. You also won't understand the opportunities you are missing to support crucial business goals like innovation, expansion into new markets and sustainability.

Perceptions, actions and structures are interrelated. Just as feelings on their own do not provide a clear picture, nor do actions or organizational processes on their own. You could have a number of inclusive systems in place, but an employee could still feel excluded because of their teammates' behavior. Only by assessing all three areas together is it possible to get a sense of how consistently or not your aspirations for inclusion are being fulfilled across the organization.

So, a comprehensive inclusion strategy measures not only what people feel, but also how they act, *and* whether there are organizational structures in place to design a work environment for all.

To function well, inclusion needs clear signals

Consider our analogy of the traffic roundabout or intersection. To ensure that it functions well, it's not enough to rely on individual drivers' feelings or actions. The junction must have clear signposts and road markings, so that it works in everyone's interests and accidents are avoided. The signs must be presented in a way that everyone can read and understand quickly, so that negotiating the intersection is straightforward. The road markings must be carefully maintained so they are visible even in difficult driving conditions.

All of this must be underpinned by comprehensive driver training and a wider system of laws, checks, rewards and penalties so that everyone takes responsibility for their own and other people's safety on the road. Altogether, this collection of signals and structures creates an ecosystem that sustains safe, functional traffic flow.

Take action: Build structures for inclusion

Design for all

Let's take this concept one step further, to designing for all. When structures and signals that facilitate inclusion are built in from the start, they are likely to be more effective than when added as an afterthought. Just as a physical relocation to a new office building is an opportunity to include features such as the latest environmentally sustainable technology, so an organizational design is an opportunity to integrate inclusion from the beginning.

Organizations can learn from the concept of universal design, which is designing environments to include as wide a range of people as possible. Incorporating quiet spaces into conference venues for people who need time to reflect and process, away from sensory stimulation, is just one example.

Universal design is more than making adjustments to enable access for specific people or groups. Building a ramp for wheelchairs at the side of a building, out of the way of most visitors, is an accessibility adjustment. Universal design is building an entry point with no steps, so that everyone can enter and leave easily, together.[6]

How else does this equate with designing inclusive organizations for all?

For one thing, it requires input from, and co-creation with, a wide range of people. The Centre for Excellence in Universal Design in Ireland runs workshops for a mix of people to learn from different perspectives and functions. "We invite along the end users, such as people from professional built environment bodies and people from our stakeholder groups," says the Centre's Neil Murphy. "You could have a landscape architect talking with an engineer, talking with someone who may be a wheelchair user, talking to someone whose child may have autism."[7]

Secondly, universal design brings benefits for everyone. Take the growing interest in how to design environments for people with autism spectrum disorder (ASD). Considerations include flexible space, minimizing background noise, signposting, thermal comfort, and safety features such as no sharp corners.

The same strategies "can make spaces more enjoyable for individuals who do not experience ASD," says Stuart Shell, a building scientist and architect at BranchPattern, a human-centered design consultancy in Omaha, Nebraska. "Autism-friendly design is just good architecture."[8]

Universal design is, therefore, a helpful way to think about how you design your organization to include everyone. How will you start to apply these principles to your inclusion strategy? What research do you need to do to take account of the broad spectrum of your employees? How will you ensure that people are able to choose the best setting for them to accomplish the work in hand? Which stakeholders will you invite into your inclusion design discussions?

Actions for senior leaders, middle managers and individuals

Senior Leaders

- Take time to reflect on what your organization is missing if it focuses only on feelings of inclusion.
- Initiate a formal and transparent assessment of how inclusive behaviors are at every level of the company, and what formal structures are in place.
- Make space and time to discuss with your colleagues what hidden assumptions you may be making that hinder a diverse mix of talent from progressing in the organization.

Middle Managers

- Establish a commitment to transparency in your team. Talk about how decisions are made about people and their opportunities and rewards at work.

- Ask for suggestions about how the formal processes and informal expectations that impact those decisions could be amended to yield fairer outcomes. Implement changes.
- Signal clearly that you believe everyone in your team has the potential to succeed.

Individuals
- Consider how common modes of operating (e.g. an expectation to work long hours) within your team might be limiting fairness.
- Explore these dynamics with your manager and colleagues to create change together. Avoid blaming. Focus on the opportunity to create more just processes that help the organization achieve its goals.
- Decide on ways to have these kinds of discussions regularly.

Making time: Stop an action you routinely take that doesn't create much value for the organization. For instance, install a distraction blocker for non-relevant social media sites that can divert your attention. Or audit your team's calendars to determine which repeated meetings are valuable and which could be permanently discontinued.

Try shortening one-hour meetings to 45 minutes, and short meetings to 10 minutes. Ask everyone to come prepared, both to be more productive and to respect and value each other's pre-work. This will create more time for the new actions you are taking to boost inclusion and will underline their importance.

Evaluating: Monitor and evaluate the impact your actions have on individual and team performance, and business success.

Addressing the Big Picture: While each action you take can boost inclusion, you also have to make changes to the whole ecosystem, as we have begun to show in this chapter.

Read on to discover how a comprehensive inclusion strategy takes account of each person's *whole* identity.

Notes

[1] Thau, S., Derfler-Rozin, R., Pitesa, M., Mitchell, M. S., & Pillutla, M. M. (2015). Unethical for the sake of the group: Risk of social exclusion and pro-group unethical behavior. *Journal of applied psychology, 100*(1), 98.

[2] For more on the structural barriers facing women in organizations, and how to fix them, read *Why Women Mean Business*, which Alison wrote with Avivah Wittenberg-Cox. See Wittenberg-Cox, A., & Maitland, A. (2008, 2009). *Why women mean business: Understanding the emergence of our next economic revolution.* John Wiley & Sons.

[3] Rattan, A. (2019). Speaking at the 2019 Behavioural Exchange. YouTube video titled, *Boosting diversity & inclusion featuring Aneeta Rattan, Elizabeth Linos & Frank Douglas.*

[4] Plummer, D.L. (2017, July 10). Getting to We: Inclusion is More than a Feeling. *Huffington Post.* Retrieved from https://www.huffpost.com/entry/getting-to-we-inclusion-is-more-than-a-feeling_b_5963ae96e4b09be68c00545b

[5] Rebekah Steele and Tim Galusha developed this ecosystem model in 2012, building upon earlier models they used and refined. You can read more about it in Steele, R. (2017, October 5). Sustainable, business-relevant results: An ecosystem approach to diversity and inclusion. Available from https://rebekahsteele.com/blogging

[6] Maisel, J.L. and Ranahan, M. (2017, October 30). Beyond accessibility to universal design. Retrieved from https://www.wbdg.org/design-objectives/accessible/beyond-accessibility-universal-design

[7] Centre for Excellence in Universal Design (n.d.). About our work on the built environment. Retrieved from http://universaldesign.ie/Built-Environment/

[8] Shell, S. (n.d.). Why buildings for autistic people are better for everyone. Forte Building Science. Retrieved from https://network.aia.org/HigherLogic/System/DownloadDocumentFile.ashx?DocumentFileKey=3fff74f0-6418-8e5f-00ed-4ebeb38eabd8&forceDialog=0

CHAPTER 5

More than Marginalized Groups

Chapter 5 Sections

Inclusion is about marginalized groups

Inclusion is also about everyone

- Taking care with the terms we use

Understand: We are many things

- Interwoven patterns of exclusion
- How white men can 'show up whole'

Measure: Be inclusive about what you ask

- Uncover the whole person's experience
- TV channel benefits by taking people out of the box

Take Action: Adjust to the rich variety of people

- Actions for senior leaders, middle managers and individuals

Inclusion is about marginalized groups

IT HAS BEEN COMMON for organizations to focus their diversity and inclusion work on marginalized populations.

Typical initiatives are organized around single marginalized identities, such as special networks called 'employee resource groups' or 'affinity groups' and mentoring programs for women or ethnic minorities.

At first glance, these efforts make sense. It is a fact that there are groups of people who are systematically excluded from opportunities. This leads to persistent and pervasive negative outcomes.

Different populations face unequal advantages and disadvantages at work and in society. As we emphasized in Chapter 2, serious work is still needed to address systemic patterns that perpetuate these disparate outcomes and experiences at work and beyond.

Inclusion is also about everyone

When it comes to creating and sustaining inclusion in organizations, however, there are several problems inherent in focusing only on marginalized groups.

First, initiatives such as employee resource groups often assume that all people with a single shared identity – such as their race, sexual orientation or physical ability – face the same enablers and constraints and need the same supports. Such an approach risks putting marginalized individuals in the very boxes they are trying to break out of. Common language used, such as 'protected' groups, can be disempowering, accentuating their 'otherness' – forever outside opportunities available to the 'mainstream'.

Barriers to inclusion look different when you consider individuals' multiple dimensions. All women do not face the same biases and restrictions, for example, as these also depend on other factors such as their race or ethnicity or (dis)ability. If you concentrate only on broad identity groups, you lose sight of the complex mix within populations.

Taking care with the terms we use

Zamila Bunglawala is very close to this issue as deputy head of the Race Disparity Unit in the British Government's Cabinet Office. In a blog post, she took issue with the acronyms that are widely used by companies, government and media to refer to ethnic minority populations: 'BAME people' (Black, Asian and Minority Ethnic) or 'BME people' (Black and Minority Ethnic).

"Personally, I have never referred to my ethnicity using BAME or BME, and I don't like it when they are used to describe me," she wrote. "Like many ethnic minorities, I proudly refer to my specific ethnic identity – my background is Indian."

Bunglawala warns against terms such as 'non-White', which defines ethnic minorities only by reference to the white population. "We do not use the term 'non-Black' when describing the White group," she says.

She urges an open conversation about people's preferences. "We all have an ethnicity, so it is important that we all discuss ethnicity in a way that is appropriate, inclusive and sensitive to how ethnic groups identify themselves."[1]

We agree this would be constructive. We would add that this open conversation should include how individuals self-identify as well.

A second problem with focusing on marginalized groups is that this can leave people in the 'mainstream' population excluded. The group seen as the 'majority' can feel targeted and blamed, which is not helpful in getting them on board for change.

Moreover, there is diversity within the mainstream, or majority, population. For example, there are plenty of men who do not identify with successful, powerful, male corporate executives. If your country has a predominantly white population, there are likely to be white ethnic groups who experience routine exclusion, such as Travelers of Irish heritage in the UK.

Thirdly, focusing just on some groups risks setting up inclusion as relevant only to people who are marginalized, leading to situations where *they* are asked to find solutions to help them feel they belong. This places the onus for driving change on those who often have the least power to create it. It does little to encourage those with the greatest privilege and power to take responsibility for change.

Finally, inclusion affects everyone. It is about people in marginalized populations who regularly face disadvantages and it is about everyone else as well.

Whether we are part of mainstream or marginalized groups, and no matter what mix of advantages and disadvantages we face, we all desire to be included. As we show later in this chapter, encompassing everyone in your inclusion strategy also generates substantial business returns.

By rethinking who inclusion is for, we can enable inclusion for everyone.

Understand: We are many things

Think of all the elements that make up your own identity – your gender, race, age, abilities, profession, personality preferences, and more. You are not just one of these. Rather, it is the coming together of the different parts of you that makes you who you are. These different elements can become more or less pronounced over time and in different contexts. Think about how your sense of who you are may have changed from a decade ago.

If you group people by a single identity, you get an incomplete picture. This picture can also be misleading. For example, when a company runs analysis of its female workforce as a single group, it misses potentially critical variances within this diverse group of people related to their race, how old they are, their relationship status, their expertise, whether they are introverted or extraverted and so on.

Here is one person's thoughtful expression of her many identities. Dr Alice Maynard, a strategic adviser on inclusive practice and a wheelchair user, describes herself this way: "I'm an older, straight, white, British, disabled, Christian woman. Mostly, I just think of myself as disabled. I think that's because of the stereotype of disabled people as asexual.

"I'm trying increasingly to think of myself as a woman. That may sound strange, but if you're disabled everything else often recedes in the face of it.

"These days, being older is also important to me. I wasn't supposed to live past five and then twentyish and then fortyish and then the medical profession gave up trying to predict. And I'm acutely aware that, given my heritage, I am bound to be deeply grounded in whiteness but that is not, for me, an important part of my identity – more something I work to counter the impact of."[2]

So, it is important in any inclusion strategy to take into account that people are more than a single identity.

Interwoven patterns of exclusion

It's also crucial to recognize that the marginalization of individuals and groups comes from many directions.

Experts in 'intersectionality' point to the interconnectedness of sexism, racism, homophobia, xenophobia and other patterns that present barriers to opportunity and privilege. This framework is helpful in tackling exclusion and building more compassionate and successful organizations and societies.

It can be useful to seek inspiration from the arts when considering how to address issues like these inside organizations.

Novelist Chimamanda Ngozi Adichie's writing and speaking about *The Danger of a Single Story* have made a big impact in helping people understand that lives are composed of various intersecting threads. Her TED talk has been seen by over 20 million viewers. As she says, focusing on only a single story about another person or country can lead to a critical misunderstanding.[3]

Bernardine Evaristo was joint winner of the 2019 Booker Prize for her unique 'fusion fiction' novel *Girl, Woman, Other*, in which she follows the interwoven lives and struggles of 12 people in Britain, mainly black and female, of different ages, classes, sexualities and occupations. Black women tend to be portrayed in wider literature through a single lens of 'angry and aggressive', so this book is refreshingly different, one Evaristo fan told the BBC's Front Row arts program. Evaristo responded: "I wanted to have a broad range of black British womanhood. But there are a lot of black British women, so no single book is ever definitive. We are many things and all things... I think we are all enmeshed in this world together."[4]

Each individual life is made up of multiple identities and experiences. Intersectionality is specific to how social patterns of discrimination converge to influence the experiences of marginalized people (e.g. how black women in the US experience pay discrimination linked to the intersections of their race and gender). Multidimensionality recognizes that none of us can be easily divided into discrete parts.

Understanding that each individual is comprised of a distinctive collection of identities makes it possible to advance inclusion more accurately, effectively and also generously. Applying this to your understanding of identity helps you to see the tremendous diversity within broad populations (e.g. among men). It helps you to anticipate that people can be affected by exclusionary practices or behaviors in relation to an element of their identity and/or life experiences, even when they are also members of a dominant group. From this perspective, it is clear that none of us is immune from the experience of exclusion.

> Limiting people to a single identity is not just incomplete. It is also misleading.

How white men can 'show up whole'

An ongoing challenge for diversity and inclusion in the Western world is how to get white men on board. White men have typically dominated companies' top echelons. So their acceptance of responsibility for partnership and enthusiasm for changing the status quo are crucial. The buy-in of white male middle managers and individual contributors is important too.

Downplaying a stigmatized part of one's identity to fit into the mainstream, a practice known as 'covering', occurs more frequently within marginalized populations. However, 45 per cent of straight white men also reported 'covering' in research carried out by Professor Kenji Yoshino with Deloitte. The range of identity aspects that they 'cover' includes age, mental disability or illness, religion and socio-economic background. Straight white men have often been left out of inclusion initiatives. Here are two perspectives from white men on ways to address this.

Nathan Roberts is chief executive of A Band of Brothers, a mentoring organization that supports young men in the UK criminal justice system to make the transition into adulthood free of crime and full of purpose and connection. He is also a leadership consultant in large companies, spending a lot of time with senior male executives.

"Men often believe they have to act and be a certain way when they're in the workplace," he says. "They're not inclusive of parts of themselves that show up when they're in a private context. They exclude their inner feminine, caring, and connected natures [at work]. To draw men into the conversation, you have to ask them what would be the value of them being able to show up whole.

"What doesn't work is anything that shames men, whether it's about their attitude on ethnicity or about gender. It will instantly have them going into lockdown. When men connect with their emotions, which takes more time, that's where change is possible."

He says senior leaders in his experience often have "huge deficits of self-esteem and identity", having been restricted by the 'tunnel vision' of believing their sole objective is to achieve success in a corporate role.

"The conversation with a male Board or executive team needs to begin with 'What do men do really well?' and acknowledging these things. Generally as human beings we are in a more positive place when we're acknowledged for what we do well. Then we can ask the question: 'Ok, what do men do less well? And as a Board or team, what might we be missing out on by not inviting in people who can do these things well, and by not inviting in the part of ourselves that could do these things well? How might that unlock our performance as an organization?'"

Chris Parke is CEO of Talking Talent, a gender diversity practice that provides coaching services to new parents and their managers. He says it can be daunting to be a male advocate of gender equality because some men don't see this as a serious business issue and some believe that it is bad news for men.

"To deal with potential hostility, male advocates may benefit from mentoring or coaching and a support network is essential," he wrote in a thoughtful blog post about his own experience. "We have to recognize that it takes a big shift for men to move from verbal support to active and public advocacy, because in doing so they risk being judged by both a female audience and male majority. We also have to accept that those new to the cause might not get all of the language or messaging exactly right. The fear of getting it wrong is far more dangerous, as it might stop potential male advocates speaking out at all."[5]

Measure: Be inclusive about what you ask

Many companies use demographic analyses to better understand inclusion and exclusion experiences of different employee groups. For example, analyses of responses to an engagement survey's inclusion-related questions may be examined according to race, gender, age, (dis)ability, education level, etc.

This approach is common and can provide some broad insights. It can be useful in spotting patterns – for example, senior employees may report feeling more included than junior employees do – meriting further investigation.

But it is also incomplete and can be misleading.

Reducing people to single categories (e.g. man/woman) sets you up to ignore the tremendous diversity *within* groups (e.g. black gay men, white women over 40, white men living with autism, or young, working class introverts). Looking at identity in silos severely limits your ability to understand the experiences of the multifaceted people comprising your organization.

We know that every person is more than a single identity. We also know that experiences of inclusion or exclusion are linked to overlapping identities that make up the *whole* of each person. A comprehensive inclusion strategy considers differences not just between groups but also within groups and within each individual. It avoids superficial and misguided one-size-fits-all responses.

Better insights provide greater direction on how to improve.

Uncover the whole person's experience

At this point, you may be wondering: how will focusing on *everyone* help me to understand the different experiences of the company's under-represented, underserved and marginalized people, compared to each other and to those in the mainstream?

While we see some value in spotting large patterns across identity groups, we recommend that organizations dig deeper with their assessment to obtain a more complete understanding of what needs to change.

Our statement with multiple-choice answers below overcomes the limitations of standard demographic silos and is structured to better access this complexity.

I would like this organization to address barriers to my inclusion related to (select all that apply):

- ☐ My age
- ☐ My gender
- ☐ My sexual orientation
- ☐ My education
- ☐ My race
- ☐ My ethnicity
- ☐ My culture
- ☐ My beliefs
- ☐ My socioeconomic background
- ☐ My ability/disability
- ☐ My primary language
- ☐ My position along the introvert-extravert continuum
- ☐ My role
- ☐ Other [open text box]
- ☐ Not Applicable

Inviting individuals to share their experience across a fuller composite of their identity, this response list provides richer information than the conventional demographic approach.

This matters in two key ways. First, directly asking individuals to define, *for themselves*, how they feel excluded helps organizations to avoid making assumptions about people's experiences. Instead of breaking down responses according to separate demographic categories and jumping to conclusions about what is going on, this formula provides information that captures the nuances of real lives.

While some findings may line up with your assumptions, your organization may discover that other dynamics matter to employees more, or less, than expected. This should lead you to probe further via focus groups or in-depth discussions with respondents.

Second, the resulting insights from this additional investigation can inform more relevant and specific action. Many organizations create employee resource groups (ERGs) to address the needs of single identity groups such as women, those from racialized communities or people with disabilities. Structured this way, ERGs fail to consider the differences within these identity silos (e.g. the needs of indigenous women vs. indigenous men, or variability within these groups related to age). Our approach encourages organizations to consider how to address the blend of *multiple* dimensions affecting inclusion.

There is a clear opportunity to develop new approaches here. In our work, we hear organizations talking about these ideas but few are yet bringing them to life in their inclusion strategies. It requires a fundamental mind shift away from discrete identity categories and a commitment to reframe your strategy to ensure you are taking people's multidimensional identities into account.

At least part of the reason for doing this is self-interest. Individuals' motivation, engagement and performance can suffer if they feel marginalized by the norms that an organization uses to define and categorize employees, according to research published in Harvard Business Review. The authors add: "To younger generations of workers, who are more likely to view self-fashioned identities as the 'norm', a traditional organizational approach can make a company appear out of touch." [6]

Addressing the whole of people's identities may sound like the right thing to do, even if it seems a bit more complicated than what companies have been doing. It isn't just the right thing, though. It can also bring substantial business benefits, as this case study demonstrates.

TV channel benefits by taking people out of the box

All That We Share is a short video made by TV2, a Danish government-owned television channel, which went viral in 2017. If you haven't seen it, we recommend you watch it.[7]

The film, which promotes inclusive programming in divisive times, is itself one of the most shared ads ever. Its simple but powerful message: we put other people in boxes, based on our kneejerk reactions. Are they like us or not? Friendly or threatening? Powerful or pitiable? When we are willing to meet the whole person behind our caricature of them, we find more in common than we think.

What if your organization put out a message that touched millions of people? What would it say? What impact would it have, internally as well as externally?

According to the creators of All That We Share, media coverage around the world generated PR worth about $100m for TV2. Within a few months of release, over two-thirds of Danes were familiar with the station's message. Viewers translated it into more than 30 languages. Each time a new part of the world began sharing the film, it revived attention in Denmark.[8]

The story of *All That We Share* demonstrates how companies can achieve their business goals and benefit from a big boost to their brand and reputation by embracing the power of everyone. The marketing narrative was experimental and bold. But what's crucial here is that it was not just a 'nice to do'. It arose directly out of the new strategy of inclusive programming and tested whether that strategy would succeed with viewers. TV2 connected its purpose – to be a channel for everyone – with its strategy and its advertising output, with staggering results.

The link to business strategy is critical. It's all very well for organizations to aspire to have an inclusive culture. Experience demonstrates that they will struggle to make sustainable progress unless they are clear about how it will help them to address their current challenges and reach their goals. Naturally blending inclusion into business priorities is a key to success.

Take action: Adjust to the rich variety of people

Actions for senior leaders, middle managers and individuals

Senior Leaders

- When making choices that affect workers, consistently ask if all are included, if all will benefit (and no one will be harmed). Ask "Who have we inadvertently left out?"
- What adjustments can you make to give employees greater autonomy and choice?
- Carve out time to work with other leaders to integrate these criteria formally into all decision making.

Middle Managers

- Ask your team to share how each of them prefers to work (e.g. morning/evening person; solo/collaborator; quiet/stimulating environment; preliminary chit-chat/straight to the point).
- Make time to discuss how you can adjust meetings and working relationships to take these different preferences into account to accomplish shared goals more

effectively. How can you cater to each worker in personalized ways when feasible?

Individuals

- Next time you are part of a joint project, start by asking your colleagues how they work best and inform them of your own preferences.
- Share your learning from this experience with your manager and broader team.
- Drawing on this knowledge, co-create ways to improve the efficiency of joint projects.

By now, you should be making progress and seeing some changes.

Congratulations!

Making time: By discontinuing any unimportant routines, you'll have more time to practice actions that cultivate inclusion. Remember to stop doing anything that undermines your efforts to elevate inclusion.

Evaluating: Continue monitoring and evaluating the impact your actions are having on individual, team, and business performance.

Addressing the big picture: If you have started to put suggested actions into play, you will have noticed the difference they make. Remember that your organization must complement individual action with systemic changes across the organization.

Read on to learn about our '10 Enablers of Inclusion' – the core components that have to be in place in an inclusive work environment.

Notes

[1] Bunglawala, Z. (2019, July 8). Please, don't call me BAME or BME! *Civil Service Blog, Gov UK*. Retrieved from https://civilservice.blog.gov.uk/2019/07/08/please-dont-call-me-bame-or-bme/

[2] Maynard, A. (2019, October). Dr. Alice Maynard speaking at an International Women's Forum UK event in London

[3] Adichie, N. (2009). The danger of a single story, TED Global 2009. Retrieved from https://www.ted.com/talks/chimamanda_adichie_the_danger_of_a_single_story?utm_campaign=tedspread&utm_medium=referral&utm_source=tedcomshare

[4] BBC (2019, October 2). BBC Radio 4 Front Row arts program.

[5] Parke, C. (2018, November 23). Between clubhouse and gender diversity conference. *Talking Talent*. Retrieved from https://www.talking-talent.com/en/between-clubhouse-and-gender-diversity-conference

[6] Humberd, B.K., Clair, J., & Rouse, E. (2020, January 24). Employee demographics don't have to be at odds with employees' identities, *HBR*. Retrieved from https://hbr.org/2020/01/employee-demographics-dont-have-to-be-at-odds-with-employees-identities

[7] TV2 Denmark (2017, January 27). All That We Share. Retrieved from https://youtu.be/jD8tjhVO1Tc

[8] We Love Ad (n.d.). All That We Share Overview. Retrieved from http://www.welovead.com/en/works/details/f0fwgnoEm

CHAPTER 6

More than 'Belonging' – 10 Enablers

Chapter 6 Sections

The easy allure of 'belonging' …

… is not a panacea

Understand: inclusion goes wider and deeper

Our 10 enablers of inclusion

- Creating connection, opportunity and common cause

Measure: Weave in the 10 enablers

- Questions about transparency
- Questions about participation
- Ways to practice the inclusion enablers

Take Action: Use the 10 enablers

- Actions for senior leaders, middle managers and individuals

The easy allure of 'belonging'…

IT IS FASHIONABLE to see 'belonging' as the next big thing for diversity and inclusion. This view has become so prevalent that some companies are now talking of swapping the terms diversity and inclusion for 'belonging'.

The allure of a catch-all term is powerful in the field of complex human behavior. Given how vague some leaders still are about what constitutes inclusion, we understand this. The idea of 'belonging' appeals to our human desire to be part of a group. It's a feeling we all know. For busy executives, the apparent simplicity of this concept must be welcome.

It would be a mistake, however, to become mesmerized by the buzzword of 'belonging'. We doubt that it provides the clarity you need about the different building blocks of an inclusive work environment, how to detect gaps in the system, or how to measure progress towards desired outcomes.

At a panel discussion titled 'Fostering Belonging at Work' at The Wharton School, University of Pennsylvania, the moderator, Stephanie Creary, asked: "What is this 'belonging' thing all about? Do we really need a new word?"[1]

The panelists from a range of companies responded by talking about the importance of challenging discrimination, leaders setting the tone, executives being allies for single-identity employee groups, ensuring that all voices are heard, connecting workers in global virtual teams, and encouraging storytelling by employees from different backgrounds.

Although the topic was 'belonging', they could just as well have been talking about inclusion, and the steps they currently take to cultivate it.

...is not a panacea

Belonging, therefore, seems to be just another word to describe inclusion. What's more, it provides only a partial view of what inclusion is. And there is a risk that focusing on belonging muddies the waters for those who want to make serious progress.

Why? For one thing, belonging is an outcome, not an input. It is about how people feel – whether, for example, they feel respected and valued for who they are and able to be themselves at work.

It suffers from the same limitations that we set out in Chapter 4's More than feelings: you cannot understand and measure belonging, or inclusion, simply by asking people how they feel. Asking if they feel they belong tells you nothing about how they behave towards others, or what specifically needs to change to make the work environment more open to everyone.

Secondly, 'belonging' can sometimes be in direct conflict with inclusion. People often feel their greatest sense of belonging when they are in a group that is similar to them, with shared backgrounds, demographics, outlooks, and interests. At the extreme, intolerance of outsiders can create a powerful sense of togetherness and belonging.

Thirdly, there are circumstances in which 'belonging' insinuates ownership. In the context of historic and modern slaveries, this interpretation of belonging, with its connotations of bondage, directly opposes the principle of being inclusive. Moreover, in some cultures marriage is considered ownership not partnership.

"I'm concerned when we focus on new terms like 'belonging' to describe a problem instead of addressing the real issue with steps that focus on our behavior and the processes, systems, and policies we work by," says May Snowden, life mastery coach, D&I thought leader, and founder and CEO of Snowden and Associates. "Rather than spending our time coming up with new terms to describe the problem, let's decide to live as if we believed that we are all valuable human beings in our thoughts, words, and behavior."

Understand: Inclusion goes wider and deeper

To cultivate inclusion, we have to work at it every day, intentionally inviting alternative perspectives and seeking out people who are different from us. We also have to build the cohesive organizational structures that create an inclusive setting.

Companies need to know what difference inclusion makes to people's lives, to performance, to customers and to achieving the organization's goals. Most are failing to capture any of that right now. At a 2018 meeting of international D&I executives, 71% reported measuring inclusion by inserting a few questions into their companies' much longer employee engagement survey.[2] Yet inclusion is at least as multi-faceted as engagement, and should be treated as such.

These limited questions offer only a small perspective of a much bigger force. To address this force comprehensively, we must go both deeper and wider.

There is growing interest from companies in the overlap between engagement and inclusion and their related impact on the employee experience. A report by The Conference Board, titled 'DNA of Engagement: The Intersection of Engagement and Inclusion'[3], suggests three actions to strengthen alignment between the two:

- Creating a shared understanding of engagement and inclusion across an organization. This can involve identification of behavior that supports both engagement and inclusion, communication about the meaning and importance of these concepts, and discussion about related opportunities and challenges.

- Setting up strategic collaboration between engagement and inclusion through governance structures, shared resources, communication and wider ownership of common priorities.

- Measuring both consistently, for example by measuring many components of both disciplines, and sharing accountability for measurable results.

One way you might approach this is with a *comprehensive* inclusion survey alongside your engagement survey. Surveys are often the default method. However there are other methods that produce deeper insights. Whether you use surveys, focus groups, coaching, every day feedback or a combination of these and other methods, the important point is to take account of all the elements of inclusion addressed in this book.

In our research and design work, we have created over 100 questions that combine information gathering and learning. Some are shared in this book. We have also devised a questionnaire aimed specially at senior leaders. (See the Measure sections of Chapters 7 and 8.)

We also recommend co-creating your inclusion insights, strategy and actions. (See Chapter 8, What does co-creation look like?)

Our 10 enablers of inclusion

In our search for more effective ways to understand, measure and act on inclusion, we looked at studies across a wide range of topics including health and wellbeing, education, social exclusion, working conditions and environmental sustainability.

Based on the knowledge we gleaned from these different areas, and our own considerable work with organizations around the world, we have identified 10 core components, or 'inclusion enablers'. As a cohesive set, they broaden your opportunities to harness people's collective superpower.

As many of these enablers are interdependent, we have clustered them under three headings:

Connection: Inclusion is about how people connect with one another. Are we open to the ideas of others who are different from us? Do we respect people across differences and feel respected by them, even when this takes us out of our comfort zone? Is there an environment of trust where good intentions are assumed?

Opportunity: Inclusion is about access to information, opportunities, and influence. Is everyone treated fairly and provided with the opportunity to learn, advance and contribute? Is there transparency about how decisions are made, goals selected, and progress achieved? Do people have choice about how they accomplish objectives?

Common cause: Inclusion is about how people work together to achieve goals. Do we provide that opportunity to others? Is power distributed across the organization, or held in the hands of a few? Does everyone have the opportunity to participate in how the organization is shaped and operates? Is there an expectation and practice of supporting one another? Are people working collaboratively toward a shared purpose?

Let's look at each of these in more detail.

Creating connection, opportunity and common cause

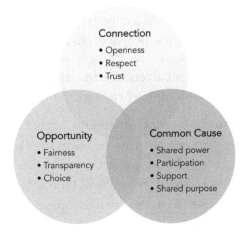

Connection: openness, respect and trust

1. Openness: We like it when people are open to hearing our views, especially if they are curious about how those views might be different from theirs. It can be a surprise to be invited to share our experience by someone with an opposing position – a surprise that can cause us to review our own thinking. None of us has a monopoly on knowledge. When we are open to different perspectives, experiences and ways of working, we learn more things faster, and we are likely to produce better ideas and solutions. But it takes intention, constant practice, and a supportive environment to stay open to difference.

2. **Respect:** We want to be treated with respect for our ideas, our work and who we are. When we are respected, we feel more motivated and engaged and are more likely to make an extra effort for the organization and to talk enthusiastically about it to others. We are more likely to contribute our ideas, enabling the creativity that companies need to succeed. We are also more likely to respect others and help them succeed. A persistent effort and a supportive environment are required.

3. **Trust:** In a trusting environment, people generally assume that others have good intentions towards them, as well as towards business goals. We feel safe to be who we are, to express our views, contribute our ideas and experiment without fear that others will undermine us or exclude us for being different. We can work to achieve common goals, rather than wasting energy on infighting, unproductive competitiveness or negative feelings such as being afraid to speak up. Being deliberate about our actions and organizational structures is necessary for trust.

Opportunity: fairness, transparency and choice

4. *Fairness:* Fairness is about ensuring that everyone can make career progress, access training and development opportunities, earn decent pay and have choice about how they work, without irrelevant obstacles based on things like age, gender, ethnicity, physical ability or socioeconomic background. It's important that people not only *feel* fairly treated, but also actually *are* fairly treated. Structures must be in place to address bias and discrimination and to ensure everyone can achieve their potential, whatever direction their talents point them.

5. *Transparency:* Hidden agendas, or the simple failure to share information, can lead to perceptions of unfairness and exclusion. If some people are left out of what's happening in the business, they can become disconnected and discouraged from being transparent with others in turn. When we know what is going on, and the intentions and reasoning behind decisions that affect us, we feel more involved and willing to contribute. We are also better equipped to take action to challenge unfair decisions and rebalance the system. Transparency takes continuous effort, and must be set up by the organization's processes and systems.

6. *Choice:* Progressive organizations recognize that people generally perform better if they are trusted to make their own choices, for example about how best to achieve their objectives. Choice is important in another way, too. Currently, some people fear speaking up or connecting with others in case they say the 'wrong' (politically incorrect or unintentionally offensive) thing. It's important that everyone can choose to bring their

'messy selves' to work, because they trust that they can have open, honest, respectful conversations in which both sides assume positive intent and learn about each other. Intentional actions and organizational processes must combine to facilitate choice.

Common cause: shared power, participation, support and shared purpose

7. **Shared power:** It may be obvious who exercises power in your organization. There may be in-groups who have access to important information, make the decisions that count, and are awarded the most exciting assignments and jobs. Sometimes, however, those in-groups are unaware of their privilege. When *we* are part of that in-group, we may imagine that we represent the norm, and that people who are different fall short. Shared power is about exercising power *with* people, not *over* them.[4] By doing so, we contribute to an environment where everyone is more willing and able to collaborate, generating better business solutions. It takes ongoing, deliberate action to bring an understanding of power dynamics into your work and into the habitual ways in which things get done in your organization. In an article in 2018, Alison set out seven requirements for changing what power looks like: singular courage; collective action; shifting the onus of change to those in power; removing trappings of power from the workplace; enabling people to speak up; adopting different styles of leadership; and ceasing public veneration of the powerful.[5]

8. **Participation:** Participation is crucial to building an inclusive work environment. It is much more than just

being part of the organization. It is about having the opportunity and resources to help define its purpose and how it operates. For some people, full participation may be hampered by how the business currently operates. It is important that everyone has a say in reviewing and changing systems to make them work for all.

9. **Support:** We thrive when we support and commit to others at work, and when we receive support and commitment back. Examples of this are checking in regularly with colleagues that they feel fully involved in joint projects, seeking and giving constructive feedback and encouragement for personal development, and stepping in to help when colleagues are overwhelmed with work or other issues. Senior leaders and managers have to model this behavior, and there must be mechanisms to support and reward people for helping others to succeed.

10. **Shared purpose:** Purpose beyond profit has become a critical goal, particularly for larger companies, as we described in Chapter 1. Like sustainability, inclusion should be a core part of a progressive organization's purpose. This is about ensuring consistency in the way people feel, how they behave and what processes are in place to support a work environment for all. Leaders' pronouncements are mirrored in everyday actions at work, and in organizational structures. For example, statements about being 'open to all' are borne out by managers discussing with team members how each prefers to work, or jobs being advertised as flexible to ensure that the most qualified people are not excluded.

Measure: Weave in the 10 enablers

Considering all of these inclusion enablers gives you a deeper understanding of how your organization is performing on specific elements of inclusion. You may, for example, already have a respectful and supportive work environment. But decision-making may be opaque, and people may be unsure whether they are fairly paid and projects are fairly allocated. You have a transparency gap. This information helps you build on success and develop targeted approaches to address the gap.

As you assess feelings, actions, and structures, you can weave these inclusion enablers into the questions you ask people at every level of the organization, the actions that you take, and the structures that you put in place.

Questions about transparency

To get started on thinking about this, here are some of our questions relating to the inclusion enabler of transparency, which you can ask people at every level of the company. You'll see that they cover feelings, actions and structures:

- Do you feel that decisions affecting your opportunities at work are well explained?
- Do senior leaders regularly take time to explain to everyone what is going on in the business?
- For decisions about who gets promoted, is the process transparent?

What are your answers to these questions about your own organization right now?

What questions would you add to help you gain further insight into the level of transparency in your organization?

Questions about participation

What about 'participation'? How would you find out whether people in your organization are truly able to participate?

Blind spots can hamper even well intentioned efforts to encourage participation. Here are some examples:

- Regularly scheduling international conference calls during the working day of the headquarters country. This diminishes the participation (and therefore the performance) of people in distant time zones, who are always obliged to call in at inconvenient hours.
- Requesting new ideas from everyone in an international organization, while expecting them to be put forward in English. This can hold back people who speak English as an additional language and are more expressive in their first language.
- Listening most to the people who talk loudest and most often. Unfortunately, this often happens. Susan Cain, author of the best-selling book *Quiet*, says "there's zero correlation between the gift of the gab and good ideas". So organizations that let this happen are missing out on valuable ideas.

Here are some of our questions relating to participation, which you can ask people at different levels of the company.

- Do you understand exactly what your contribution is to the organization's goals?
- Do managers encourage people to speak up in the way that is most comfortable for the individual?
- Is there a formal process to ensure all employees have a real say in how this organization works?

What are your answers to these questions about your own organization right now?

What questions would you add to help you gain insight into the level of participation in your organization?

Ways to practice the inclusion enablers

Through her training and practice as a facilitator and coach, Alison has discovered accessible ways to bring these enablers of inclusion out into the open.

Drawing on several programs she has completed – Co-Active Training Institute, Collective Leadership, and Conversational Intelligence® for Coaches – she facilitates teams to discuss what everyone needs from each other and from themselves to collaborate successfully.

Everyone participates, and the team agreement is not finalized until everyone is comfortable signing up to it. It's also useful to refresh your team agreement regularly. The whole process can uncover issues beneath the surface and lead to important conversations about things like respect, trust, transparency, fairness, and choice. Because everyone is invested and accountable, it can shift perceptions of power and influence.

Another inclusive process can be used at the end of meetings to enhance trust, transparency, mutual support, and shared purpose by giving everyone a voice. The LEARN exercise was devised by the late Judith E. Glaser, who describes it in her book *Conversational Intelligence*. Using the acronym, each person is invited to say what they liked, what excited them, what created anxiety, what deserved a reward (R can alternatively be for questions such as "what would you like to reframe or revise?"), and finally what needs to be done in terms of next steps.[6]

As we note throughout this book, such practices take more time. It's worth it. The investment reaps a big payback in terms of openness, trust, motivation, accountability, and shared purpose – key elements of inclusion linked to business goals and outcomes.

Take action: Use the 10 enablers

Actions for senior leaders, middle managers and individuals

Senior Leaders

- Begin a reciprocal mentorship with someone who is different from you, with a focus on helping each other become more inclusive leaders.
- Use the 10 enablers as discussion points for that development work. Consider what you can learn from this process that would be useful to incorporate as a standard part of leadership development.

Middle Managers

- Formally commit to working on all three sets of inclusion enablers – connection, opportunity, and common cause – to increase team collaboration in achieving a critical performance objective.

- Discuss how to do this with your team, work on it with a peer coaching group, and/or find someone with insight and expertise to guide you.

Individuals

- Partner with colleagues to explore which of the 10 enablers are strengths that you already consistently weave into your collective work.
- Work together on a plan to address gaps individually and as a team. Share your plan with others, and invite colleagues from other parts of the organization to join in.

Making time: You will now be in the habit of considering what to stop each time you begin a new action. What will you eliminate to make room for your fresh focus on inclusion? What old patterns need to stop so they won't jeopardize your efforts?

Evaluating: You will now be building in regular monitoring and evaluation of the impact of your actions. What effect are your actions having on individual engagement, team performance, and business success?

Addressing the big picture: Each individual can act to make a difference for inclusion. Systemic organizational changes are necessary, too.

Read on to broaden your inclusion strategy to key business relationships outside the organization.

Notes

1   Knowledge@Warton (2019, March 26). Beyond Diversity: How firms are cultivating a sense of belonging. Retrieved from https://knowledge.wharton.upenn.edu/article/belonging-at-work/

2   The Conference Board (2018, September). Poll about measuring inclusion, Joint Meeting of The Conference Board's Global D&I Executives and D&I in Business Councils, Paris, France.

3   Erickson, R., Sabattini, L., & Popiela, A. (2020). DNA of Engagement: The Intersection of Engagement and Inclusion. The Conference Board. (Manuscript in preparation).

4   The concept of exercising power with people, instead of over people, originated with Mary Parker Follett, the early 20th century American management theorist, who advocated for non-coercive power-sharing. She was also instrumental in the notions of 'win-win' and seeing diversity as a strength.

5   Maitland, A. (2018, January 26). Seven ways to change what power looks like. Retrieved from http://alisonmaitland.com/seven-ways-to-change-what-power-looks-like/

6   Glaser, J. E. (2014). *Conversational Intelligence: How great leaders build trust and get extraordinary results*. Bibliomotion. (see p. 143)

CHAPTER 7

More than the Internal Workforce

Chapter 7 Sections

Opening from the inside out

External systems affect progress

Lessons in empathy and understanding

- Bringing everyone on board for sweeping change

External stakeholders matter

Understand: The risks and benefits

- Cleaning Schiphol Airport collectively

Measure: The quality of stakeholder ties

- Benefits of hiring refugees

Take Action: Fulfil unmet needs

- Mental health campaign extends inside and out
- Actions for senior leaders, middle managers and individuals

Opening from the inside out

MOST ORGANIZATIONS STILL FOCUS their inclusion efforts on their internal workforce. What happens inside is important, but there's also more to an ambitious and comprehensive inclusion strategy than that.

Organizations are part of society. They impact and are impacted by what happens beyond their boundaries. Alone or in concert, large companies in particular wield huge power, influencing government policy and shaping the communities in which they operate. External systems, relationships and exchanges also influence the extent to which organizations can make change internally.

As we'll see in this chapter, forward-thinking companies are recognizing that their inclusion strategy must look outwards as well as inwards.

To make maximum progress inside your organization, you have to weave inclusion into your external relationships. You also have to look outside to learn from the best initiatives in society.

External systems affect progress

Consider these questions about external systems and policies that can support or hinder inclusion in your own company:

- Does public policy support inclusion? Are LGBTQIA[1] rights protected by law? Is racial pay equity required? Are refugees welcome?
- What legal sanctions exist for discrimination, abuse, harassment, bullying, trolling and other extreme forms of exclusion? Are they applied consistently?
- Are essential resources such as clean water, power supplies and communications technology distributed equitably to your employees, customers, and communities?
- Is employment retraining in place for those whose work is being displaced by technology?
- Are there partnerships with justice systems to train or hire people who have lived in prison?

- Do schools teach children the importance of inclusive behavior and the value of difference?
- Does everyone have equal access to education?
- Do business schools teach executives what inclusion is and how to measure it?

Expanding the Ecosystem model we introduced in Chapter 4, the diagram below shows the economic, social and environmental factors that organizations should take into account in designing and implementing a comprehensive inclusion strategy.

Inclusion Ecosystem

Connective Sustainability

Social Sustainability

Leadership Strategy

People Capability

Org Structure

Business Strategy

Inclusion

Business Results

Metrics & Rewards

Processes

Individual Assumptions/ Behaviors

Market Sustainability

Environmental Sustainability

Economic Sustainability

Steele's expanded Ecosystem Model[2]

Social sustainability involves education/training, public policy, healthcare, social welfare, housing, justice, safety

Environmental sustainability involves access to clean energy, water and sanitation, equitable resource consumption, climate action choices

Economic sustainability involves productivity, diversification, innovation, employment, entrepreneurship

Market sustainability involves investors, suppliers, partners, customers or clients, end users, communities

Connective sustainability involves media, technology, transportation, communications

To give a couple of examples:

Government regulations can make a big difference to the extent of inclusion inside companies. If legislation encourages all parents to take leave to care for children, there is a supportive external environment for your internal drive to help ensure gender isn't a barrier to leadership development and opportunities. If legislation requires gender pay gap reporting, as introduced in countries such as France, Germany and the UK, this increases scrutiny and adds urgency to organizational initiatives for change. Beyond parental leave or equal pay, a government's position on free speech can also promote or hinder people speaking up with different ideas and perspectives in organizations.

What happens in education systems also feeds into behavior at work, supporting or undermining efforts to break down barriers and challenge assumptions relating to difference. Roots of Empathy (RoE) is an international organization that has been running classroom programs for over 20 years, helping children to develop empathy, emotional intelligence and social connections that foster inclusion.[3]

Children 'get it', but adults do not always do so, or they forget it, says RoE founder and president Mary Gordon. Yet it is crucial for success at work. "The ability to attune to another person, to be able to take their perspective and understand their feelings, is a super highway of connectivity that enhances any business relationship," she says.[4]

Indeed, empathy at work is positively related to job performance, according to research by the Center for Creative Leadership, analyzing data from 6,731 managers in 38 countries. It found that managers who showed more empathy towards their direct reports were seen by their bosses as better performers at their jobs.[5]

Lessons in empathy and understanding

To build connections and collaboration for an inclusive work environment, you have to touch people's hearts as well as their minds.

Social initiatives hold lessons from which organizations can gain inspiration. Here's one example, relating to the divisions opened up by the UK referendum on leaving the European Union. Residents from Boston, Lincolnshire, the highest 'leave' voting area, and Lambeth, London, the highest voting area for remaining in the EU, connected to understand each other's positions on Brexit. By spending time talking, listening and eating together, they gained empathetic understanding and became comfortable with each other. As one resident reported, they recognized they have 'more in common'.[6]

If we can also change our *inner* conversations, it becomes easier to have productive conversations with other people across differences, as Alison explained in an article about how the 'More in Common' initiative translates to working life.[7]

We can learn a lot from children, too. During our research, we came across a short video from CBeebies, the BBC's television channel for under-sixes, about how young children view difference. "What makes you two different?"

the interviewer asks pairs of friends of different ethnic origins. They ponder. Then one boy pipes up: "I used to not like lettuce, but now I like lettuce," and his friend says: "I do *not* like lettuce at all."

Two other little boys who have struggled to think of any differences finally come up with something. One of the boys points at his friend and says he is better at the game of 'tig', also known as 'tag' or 'it'. His friend replies: "And Matthew's good at staying in den [home base]."

The interviewer asks the same question of a girl in a wheelchair, while her friend jiggles on the edge of a chair next to her. "Lucy loves tomato sauce, and I do like it, but I don't love it as much as Lucy," she says.[8]

Preferences in food and games are much more significant to these young children than visible differences in skin color or mobility. They are not yet conscious of the meanings, sometimes awkward or threatening, that society imposes on them.

Food and games are good topics to bring people together at any age. Inclusion doesn't have to be hard if we tap into our childlike curiosity and reconnect with what we have in common as human beings and how our differences make our lives richer and more worthwhile.

Bringing everyone on board for sweeping change

Tostan, a community development NGO working mainly in West Africa, facilitates a whole-system approach to help communities bring about remarkable change across education, health, environment, governance, economic empowerment, gender and social norms in just three years.

With a vision of dignity for all, the Tostan model is human rights-based, respectful, inclusive, holistic and sustainable. It keeps rural communities in charge of their own futures. For example, information is shared in a non-judgmental and participatory way, using local languages.

The program has reached more than 5 million people across eight African countries, empowering women into leadership and public office and communities into committing publicly to ending female genital cutting and child marriage. The video *Walk on My Own* describes the program.[9]

Tostan has been willing to learn. In its early days, it found that its lessons on women's rights created opposition, with men closing down its centers. So it redesigned its approach to focus on people's rights and equitable decision-making, and successfully brought men on board. Rather than being positioned as foes, "the men just want to be included," said founder Molly Melching.[10]

When Rebekah learned about Tostan in 2009, she recognized many validating similarities between the organization's approach and the way she works with corporations to advance inclusion. She chose to get involved as co-founder and President of Tostan Canada, which provided her with a rich path to learning more from this leading NGO while working to help expand its impact.

> What initiatives does your company support to equip future workers with the skills to connect, collaborate and resolve conflicts constructively?

How are you improving your inclusion strategy by learning from the best initiatives out there?

External stakeholders matter

As well as broader social dynamics, it is important to consider the perspectives and needs of non-employees who are intricately connected to your company. Nurturing strong relationships with these external stakeholders – the people who are your customers, suppliers, contract workers, investors and regulators – is more important than ever in a world where feedback is instant and often highly visible.

A key requirement for companies in many countries today is to be able to provide evidence of a diverse supply chain, as well as diversity in the workforce and leadership ranks. Extending your *inclusion* strategy to suppliers, contractors, investors and other stakeholders will take you a step further, building and deepening key connections, trust, loyalty and responsiveness.

Here are two external groups you could consider right away:

'On demand' workforce: Companies are increasingly reliant on a flexible supply of 'on demand' workers to provide the solutions and services they need – from highly paid consultants and PhD-equipped researchers to virtual administrators, drivers and cleaners. HR software company, Zenefits, includes contingent and part-time workers in a full range of employee-related investments, such as benefits, learning and development and flexibility.

This is one way they ensure gig economy workers can be just as included as full-time employees.[11]

Does your company's inclusion strategy extend to this growing 'on demand' workforce? Or is it confined to employees on your payroll, and perhaps even just to 'top talent'? Do you do the basics, paying contractors promptly? Do you offer benefits to your 'on demand' workers, or include them when you're consulting employees on strategy, new products, or employment perks? Do you involve them in social occasions? If not, can you truly call yourself an inclusive organization?

Investors: Shareholders are demonstrating greater interest in issues like gender balanced and ethnically diverse leadership, and pay equality. At the same time, corporate reporting is evolving beyond just financial capital. The integrated reporting movement, founded on systems thinking, challenges organizations to consider the interaction between their business model and the resources and relationships that it affects and on which it relies. This broader perspective is designed to enhance understanding and decision-making about how value is created.[12]

Does your organization's inclusion strategy take investors into account? Are you speaking with investors regularly about progress towards your inclusion goals and seeking their input on the value that inclusion creates? Could you be missing out on potential investors because of the way you address, or fail to address, inclusion?

Understand: The risks and benefits

As we saw above, the strength or weakness of external systems will inevitably affect your ability to build and sustain a fully inclusive environment at work. Cultivating inclusion will be harder if your organization operates in societies that do not consider everyone's human rights to be equal and inviolable.

We pointed out in Chapter 2 that many organizations are also concerned about employee wellbeing and productivity amid the fallout from external acts of violence against groups perceived as 'different'.

If your company profits from targeting products at underserved populations, does it also take a stand when public discourse singles out those same populations for violent physical or verbal attack?

An organization's work on inclusion cannot be limited to internal strategies alone. It has to address external forces head on. That may mean speaking out and lobbying governments for change, or supporting non-profit initiatives to tackle social exclusion, or forming partnerships with external experts to find better ways to address problems affecting your employees, customers and wider society. Here are two more examples.

Advertising: An inclusion strategy falls short if it does not extend beyond organizational boundaries. It also increases risk. One international bank damaged its internal drive to recruit and promote women and marginalized ethnic groups when it ran a series of external advertisements depicting only able-bodied, athletic white men.

By contrast, Procter & Gamble has galvanized its internal inclusion efforts with bold videos highlighting biases and challenging stereotypes based on gender, race, and more. Marc S. Pritchard, chief brand officer, sees the connections between highlighting bias, advancing inclusion, and doing good for the P&G business. This comes to life in ads such as We See Equal, The Talk, and The Look, which are part of a deliberate strategy focused on ensuring purposeful media that is both a "force for good and a force for growth".[13]

External workers: Companies that fail to ensure their contract workers are fairly treated can find themselves in the firing line. Susana Benavides, a cleaner at the flagship Topshop store in London, made headlines when she was awarded compensation by an employment tribunal for unfair dismissal. Cleaning agency Britannia terminated her employment because of her role in leading a trade union protest against 'poverty pay' outside the shop. Subsequently given a voice in the *Guardian* newspaper, Benavides wrote about how "I suffer twice" – as a migrant facing language barriers and as a woman, working and caring for others.[14]

It makes sense to extend inclusion outwards, for business as well as ethical and sustainability reasons. Leaving people out and alienating them creates fertile ground for division and disruptive action, which in turn undermines economic stability and a healthy environment in which business can thrive. It does not have to be that way. Bringing everyone in and giving them a voice promotes collaboration to produce better outcomes, whether business, social, environmental or a combination of these.

Here's a different story.

Cleaning Schiphol Airport collectively

Amsterdam Schiphol is one of the world's oldest airports, having commenced civilian flights in 1920. It is also very clean. When Alison travelled through in 2019, she noticed an unusual poster in the washroom. It welcomes passengers in five languages and at the bottom has a photo of four cleaners from diverse backgrounds, with the caption: "We keep this Schiphol restroom clean".

Cleaners often carry out their work unnoticed and uncelebrated, so Alison was keen to find out more. As one of Europe's busiest airports, Schiphol uses four cleaning companies. In the past, the cleaners from each company operated separately and wore different uniforms. But when the airport put the contracts out to tender in 2016, it required applicants to work together in a collective agreement, to raise standards and ensure consistent quality in pursuit of Schiphol's ambition to be Europe's Preferred Airport.

The collective agreements cover inclusion and diversity, education, safety, quality and environmental goals, says Rajko Kascelan, HR manager for one of the cleaning companies, Asito, which employs 500 people at Schiphol and has a strong focus on inclusion. "If you're forced to work with each other, you can also help each other, because one company may know more about some areas than the others do."

The idea for the photo was a collective one, says Kascelan, to feature a cleaner from each company, now all wearing the same uniform but with their distinct logos – Asito, Hago, ISS, and Raggers. Many of the cleaners, who represent over 40 nationalities, have worked at the airport for 25-30 years, moving from one employer to another as contracts changed. "We wanted to give them a feeling of satisfaction about the work they do."

What difference has the public poster made to the cleaners? "They feel more pride, approval and recognition of their work," he says. "They are very important for the airport, and travelers ask them a lot of questions, like how to get to their departure gate. But cleaning is not very often celebrated."[15]

Measure: The quality of stakeholder ties

In our work with companies, we use a questionnaire to ask senior leaders about what organizational policies and processes they have to foster inclusive interactions internally and externally. We ask, for example, how they engage with a whole range of stakeholders and what impact inclusion has on a variety of outcomes including customer satisfaction and shareholder value.

Discovering the answers to these questions will help you to see where there may be gaps in your inclusion strategy and where you need to work harder to build strong relationships beyond the organization's boundaries.

Leading companies are starting to make the connections between inclusiveness on the one hand, and social and environmental sustainability on the other. The global refugee crisis is a case in point. Armed conflict, forced displacement, poverty and natural disasters are driving the crisis. Moreover, without urgent action on climate change, 143 million people could be forced to move within their countries' borders in Sub-Saharan Africa, South Asia and Latin America by 2050, according to the World Bank.[16]

Coordinated action by national governments is critical, but many different actors, including NGOs and affected communities must be part of it. Companies also have a role to play, as this case study shows.

Benefits of hiring refugees

Sodexo, the international services company, took a deliberate decision to hire refugees in recent years as a way to benefit the business and address a global crisis. Recently it committed to recruiting in Sweden, the US, Canada, France, Germany and Italy, after experience hiring in Brazil, where thousands of refugees have fled to escape persecution and violence in countries such as Haiti, Venezuela, Cuba and Syria.

Sodexo points to research showing that companies known to support refugees enjoy increased reputation, sales and recruitment. Its Brazil operation took care to prepare the ground with employees before the refugees arrived, telling them about the people who were coming and reminding staff of the company's commitment to inclusion. The company also collaborated with resettlement agencies and produced practical guides for refugees and potential employers.[17]

Teams that have welcomed refugees have reported increased morale and engagement, Sodexo reports. Refugees are often highly skilled and able to transfer skills such as languages to other employees. Rohini Anand, then head of corporate responsibility and global chief diversity officer, told us that Sodexo wanted to do more with refugees to help fill its skills gaps. "We have an incredible opportunity to increase diversity in the workplace, and to address talent gaps while doing so. There's evidence that refugees have higher retention rates. The business outcome is our main driver."[18]

Take action: Fulfill unmet needs

Partnering with specialist external organizations is a good way for businesses to advance their inclusion goals, for example by addressing societal challenges that impact not only their internal workforce but also customers and communities.

Before we look at specific actions you can take, here's an example of how this can work.

Mental health campaign extends inside and out

In 2017, António Horta-Osório, CEO of Lloyds Banking Group in the UK, instituted a resilience program for its top 200 leaders. They learned about sleep, nutrition, psychological tools and other ways to avoid mental illness. The initiative reflected the CEO's own experience six years earlier when, just months after stepping into the role, he had to take a break to recover from extreme stress and insomnia.

Insights from the program were used to develop a 'resilience portal' for everyone in the company, allowing them to assess themselves and gain practical, tailored advice to increase their resilience and wellbeing.

To challenge the stigma about disclosing mental health problems, the bank ran a social media-style competition in which more than 2,000 employees shared top tips for improving mental wellbeing. These included simple things like understanding nutrition, getting enough sleep or taking a walk during lunch breaks. This new openness continued, with some relating experiences of mental illness on the bank's internal website. Over five years, the bank says, the number of people who felt able to declare their mental health condition in the annual employee survey doubled to over 1,300.

As a way to include everyone, the mental health focus has been a unifier across the organization of 75,000 people because it touches everyone, says Fiona Cannon, whose group director role unusually combines responsible business, sustainability, and inclusion & diversity. "No matter what your background, either you or someone you know has been affected."

The bank extended the initiative outwards as well, partnering with the charity Mental Health UK. It ran an advertising campaign in 2018 called #GetTheInsideOut to open up awareness about mental ill-health and the stigma attached to it. In the videos, celebrities and non-celebrities play a version of the game 'Who Am I?' with Post-It Notes stuck on their foreheads, each with a different mental condition written on them, asking questions to guess what it might be and how people might react.[19]

Employees participated by raising funds for a specialist Mental Health & Money Advice service, provided by the charity, for customers experiencing problems. In the first two years after its launch in 2017, over 1,400 people had benefited, saving each person an average of £1,500 worth of debt, says Cannon.

Lloyds was one of 30 UK businesses and NGOs joining forces in October 2019 to sign a Mental Health at Work Commitment to promote openness, provide tools and support, and "proactively ensure work design and organizational culture drive positive mental health outcomes".

All of this underscores the link between inclusion and responsible business, says Cannon. "Inclusion is not just a human resources matter. It's a demonstration of how you're responsible as a company in the world, and with your customers as well as your colleagues."[20]

What impactful outcome would you like to achieve for your business and workforce by partnering with an expert external initiative?

Actions for senior leaders, middle managers and individuals

Senior Leaders

- Start a conversation with your board of directors about seizing opportunities to promote inclusion by addressing external stakeholders' needs. Focus on ways to do this that will have a positive impact on employee experience, team performance, product and service design, and/or reputation.
- Add progress on inclusion into your discussions with investors about Environmental, Social and Governance issues.

Middle Managers

- Actively seek input from customers about their unmet needs and potential solutions (products or services) that you can create together. Do the same with contractors and suppliers. Use this information to update and customize your inclusion processes for greater impact.

- Find ways to share joint progress that enhance your company's reputation with these stakeholders.

Individuals
- Ask your manager to devote part of each team meeting to gathering input for big upcoming decisions, so you have an active part in defining how the organization works.
- Run a session with colleagues, including support staff, where everyone shares a 'hidden talent' (e.g. speaking an additional language). Discuss how the team can use these to achieve common goals.

Making time: Remember to make room for your new actions to increase inclusion by saying No to activities that are getting in the way. This is a tool that Alison uses in coaching, when clients are embarking on a significant change. Saying Yes, and fully committing to a new action or behavior, is most effective when you say No to an old habit or practice that is holding you back. Another example might be letting go of perfection or unrealistic timelines for projects that are low priority.

Evaluating: Continue to monitor and evaluate the impact you are making on individual, team and business success.

Addressing the big picture: Continue to take action while ensuring systemic organizational changes are being implemented, too.

Read on to direct all you've learned so far into more impactful business results.

Notes

1   LGBTQIA: Lesbian, Gay, Bisexual, Transgender or Two-Spir-
    ited, Queer or Questioning, Intersexed, Asexual

2   Building upon the internal Ecosystem model co-developed with
    Tim Galusha, Rebekah Steele has expanded the model to take
    account of the broader environment.

3   Roots of Empathy: https://rootsofempathy.org

4   Gordon, M. (2018, December). The Magic Ingredient of
    Success. Retrieved from https://uk.rootsofempathy.org/the-
    magic-ingredient-of-success-empathy-and-business/

5   Gentry, W. A., Weber, T. J., & Sadri, G. (2007). *Empathy in the
    workplace: A tool for effective leadership.* A Center for Creative
    Leadership White Paper. Retrieved from
    http://www.ccl.org/leadership/pdf/research/EmpathyInThe
    Workplace.pdf

6   BBC News (2019, March 29). More in Common - how voters
    are bridging the Brexit divide. Retrieved from
    https://www.bbc.com/news/video_and_audio/headlines/477
    46311/more-in-common-how-voters-are-bridging-the-brexit-
    divide

7   Maitland, A. (2019, May 17). Bridging divides for better
    outcomes at work. Retrieved from
    http://alisonmaitland.com/bridging-divides-for-better-
    outcomes-at-work/

8   BBC Family News (2017, June 18). What makes you two
    different from each other? Retrieved from
    www.facebook.com/BBCFamilyNews/videos/1319354311433
    201/

9   Walk On My Own: The Story of Keur Simbara's
    Breakthrough for Women and Girls' Wellbeing.
    https://youtu.be/HGHtER4JHA0

10 Kristof, N.D., and Wudunn, S. (2009). *Half the sky, Turning
    oppression into opportunity for women worldwide.* New York, NY:
    Alfred A. Knopf.

11 Fulcher, J. (2019, May 15). The New World of Work: the
    'Blended' Workforce. Retrieved from
    https://thriveglobal.com/stories/the-new-world-of-work-
    blended-workforce-jay-fulcher/

12 For more information, visit the International Integrated

Reporting Council https://integratedreporting.org

[13] Myers, J. (2018, December 12). P&G's Marc Pritchard on Brands as a Force for Good, and Personal Goals. Retrieved from https://www.mediavillage.com/article/pgs-marc-pritchard-on-brands-as-a-force-for-good-and-personal-goals/ The videos included in the above are: P&G. (2017, March 1). *We See equal*. Retrieved from https://youtu.be/g6E4pfAzUCE; P&G. (2017, July 20). *The Talk:*. Retrieved from https://youtu.be/3s20ePvTaME and P&G. (2019, July 3). *The Look*. Retrieved from https://youtu.be/aC7lbdD1hq0

[14] Benavides, S. (2018, March 8). As a migrant woman I suffer twice. Part of series: Why we're striking for women's rights today. *The Guardian*. Retrieved from www.theguardian.com/commentisfree/2018/mar/08/striking-womens-rights-international-womens-day-protests-uk

[15] Interview with author (2019, September)

[16] The World Bank. (2018, March 19). Groundswell: Preparing for internal climate migration. Infographic. Retrieved from https://www.worldbank.org/en/news/infographic/2018/03/19/groundswell---preparing-for-internal-climate-migration

[17] Sodexo. (2019, May 17). *Addressing Culture and Origins across the Globe*. Available from https://www.sodexo.com/en/media/culture-origins-across-globe.html

[18] Interview with author. (2019, May).

[19] #GetTheInsideOut videos. Retrieved from https://youtu.be/y5gXneVOz8A

[20] Interview with author. (2019, September).

CHAPTER 8

Inclusion with Impact

Chapter 8 Sections

Pulling it all together for business results
- Understanding and measuring the 5 Ws

Positioning inclusion at the heart of business strategy
- Sample questions for senior leaders
- Sample questions for middle managers
- Sample questions for individuals

We need personal action, and more

What does co-creation look like?

Why Inclusion IMPACT® is distinctive

Envisaging an inclusive work environment

Pulling it all together for business results

HAVING REACHED THIS POINT, you will appreciate the importance of a comprehensive and cohesive approach to inclusion. You will also have a good idea of the risks that organizations face when they adopt only piecemeal initiatives.

Building inclusion in organizations is not an end in itself. To stay alive, it must be linked to better results for business and, ultimately, for society too. It must contribute to improved decision-making, productivity, innovation, market growth, sustainability and other outcomes we highlighted in Chapter 1 and in the examples throughout the book.

It's impossible to do that with a piecemeal approach.

To summarize, most organizations currently seek to understand and measure inclusion with only a limited view of the who, what, where, and why, as shown in the diagram below.

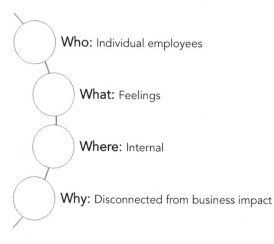

Who: Individual employees

What: Feelings

Where: Internal

Why: Disconnected from business impact

This is ineffective. Limited understanding and measurement result in limited action and results. When companies do take action, this is often confined to developing inclusive behavior in leaders and/or creating special networks for marginalized groups, sometimes supported by executive 'allies'. Many companies do not know whether their efforts are driving better results or not.

Understanding and measuring the 5 Ws

In contrast to this restricted view, using our approach challenges companies to recognize the big picture of inclusion, as shown below.

Who: Individuals, Teams, Managers, Senior Leaders

What: Feelings, Actions and Structures x 10 Enablers

Where: Internal and External

Why: Individual, Business and Social Impact

Who: Inclusion is about everyone, because everyone benefits from inclusion and everyone is responsible for making it happen. It involves senior leaders and middle managers and individuals and teams. It covers not only people who are marginalized but also people in the mainstream population.

What: Inclusion involves not just feelings, but also actions, and the structures (such as processes, written and unwritten rules, and other signals) that are needed to facilitate and sustain it. It also depends on having in place the ingredients that make it possible, encapsulated in our 10 enablers of inclusion.

Where: What's going on inside your organization is crucial. But inclusion should also apply to your dealings with external partners and stakeholders. You can learn how to strengthen inclusion internally from the best external initiatives, too.

Why: Not simply an end in itself, inclusion can contribute to wellbeing and engagement, innovation and market growth, social and environmental sustainability and other positive outcomes. Inclusion strategies need to be directly linked to results to have maximum effect for individuals, business, and society.

To these four Ws, we now add a fifth:

When: Organizations that measure inclusion typically do so as a small part of the annual employee engagement survey. However, inclusion is not something that can be achieved and then set aside, even for a short time. It is dynamic and dependent on context and experience. Individuals don't usually start out knowing themselves well, but develop and change over time as they discover who they want to be. They also come to understand themselves through relationships with others. Organizations need to take this into account. Inclusion requires intention in every moment, every interaction and every relationship.

That is why we have provided plenty of actions you can take with colleagues across and beyond your organization.

One action you could take right away is a simple self-assessment of whether you are, or are not yet, addressing each of the five Ws above. See Appendix 2 for a detailed diagram of our Inclusion IMPACT® 5Ws.

Positioning inclusion at the heart of business strategy

With this comprehensive structure in place, the work of cultivating and sustaining an environment that works for all and contributes to business success becomes more clear-cut, viable and compelling.

Inclusion is no longer perceived as a distraction from, or addition to, core business goals. Positioning it at the heart of the business strategy attracts the support necessary to drive successful outcomes including executive sponsorship, budget and resources, measurement and accountability. Simply, inclusion becomes an essential and indivisible part of an organization's focus.

To support this integration, our Inclusion IMPACT® approach typically starts with asking senior leaders how inclusion can help them achieve their current and future business goals. This quickly makes the connections clear while addressing concerns that inclusion will divert attention away from business priorities.

Sample questions for senior leaders

Our detailed Senior Leader Questionnaire asks questions such as:

- Are you measuring progress with inclusion in your organization?
- Does inclusion at your organization have a positive impact on retaining the best talent?
- Does inclusion have a positive impact on shareholder value?

- Is your organization measuring the impact of increased inclusion on retaining the best talent?
- Is your organization measuring the impact of increased inclusion on shareholder value?

Instant insights: The head of D&I at a retail company experienced two sudden insights as she completed our Senior Leader Questionnaire. First, she realized how few formal processes the company had to build inclusion into the way work regularly gets done. Second, she realized that they had a dearth of measurements about the difference inclusion makes to critical business outcomes, such as innovation, market growth and sustainability. "We really need to measure inclusion's impact on the success of our business," she said. "Your questionnaire raises and emphasizes this opportunity."

In addition to the Senior Leader Questionnaire, we also weave the business impact into questions for middle managers and individuals so that inclusion becomes ever more clearly associated with outcomes for the organization.

Sample questions for middle managers

- Are you measuring the impact of increased inclusion on your own performance?
- Are you measuring the impact of increased inclusion on innovation in your team(s)?

How middle managers answer questions like these helps to identify what is being done to promote inclusion for the business and where the gaps lie.

Sample questions for individuals

- Does your manager explicitly link hearing everyone's views with improved performance?

The answer to this indicates whether messages about the impact of inclusion on results are getting through to workers.

- Is inclusion making a difference to team performance?
- Is inclusion making a difference to problem-solving?
- Is inclusion making a difference to motivation?

These are some of the questions that can be asked as people in your organization start to take concerted action to increase inclusion. They can be tailored to specific inclusive actions, like the ones we suggest in each chapter, to dig deeper into what drives better results.

We need personal action, and more

Throughout this book, we have recommended actions for individuals at all levels in the organization. This isn't just a throwaway idea. Everyone is accountable for inclusion.

And while personal action is necessary to advance inclusion, it is not enough.

As we have argued, you need a different approach to get different results. In this spirit, one valuable and inclusive technique to help organizations achieve greater inclusion is co-creation. Bringing together a mix of individuals to tackle challenges collaboratively and achieve new solutions is particularly well suited to the work of increasing inclusion.

In contrast to conventional approaches that often separate data collection, analysis and response, co-creation can help organizations build solutions and buy-in more rapidly as it directly involves stakeholders in an experience that combines inclusion learning, assessment and action.

What does co-creation look like?

Informal team: There is a simple way to get started with co-creation. Make a practice of meeting with a mix of colleagues to discuss barriers to inclusion and opportunities to address them. Engage with people from a range of roles and from an array of departments. Think about inviting stakeholders beyond those who work in your organization. This practice can help challenge assumptions about inclusion and broaden thinking about potential solutions. To achieve value from this informal process, it's critical to commit to moving the strongest ideas forward. You'll need to gain support to implement them, at least as a pilot, and evaluate their impact.

Formal task force: Organizations can take co-creation a step further by commissioning a task force with the formal responsibility to collaboratively generate solutions to grow inclusion. In contrast to the informal approach detailed above, this demonstrates greater commitment to change. It increases the potential for action through formal direction, support, and accountability for bringing ideas to life. As task force members bring their complementary experiences, identities, and perspectives to the work of designing and implementing solutions together, the *indivisible whole* of inclusion becomes clearer.

Inclusion design lab: An organization can take co-creation to the next level by facilitating experiences specifically structured to examine *and* create ways to enhance inclusion rapidly. Rebekah's signature D&I Breakthrough Labs use design thinking to harness the power of diversity in an intentionally inclusive setting. These labs integrate D&I principles, human-centred design thinking, and the creativity of the arts as they engage a mix of people in co-creating bold new ways to bring inclusion to life in an organization.[1]

In contrast to informal teams or formal task forces, the lab experience allows participants to rapidly and simultaneously learn about the whole of inclusion, to explore and assess the current state of inclusion, to commit to individual action, and to move directly to the collaborative design of innovations to advance inclusion at work. Because people are more likely to support change that they create, the lab approach can lead participants to become powerful and on-going agents of change.

Sticking with the status quo is risky.

Standard approaches to understanding and addressing inclusion are incomplete and inefficient.

Are you bold enough to embrace a different approach?

Why Inclusion IMPACT® is distinctive

Taken together, all these elements add up to a comprehensive, actionable and sustainable approach to inclusion. In addition to prioritizing results, the other key elements are: in-depth measurement; practical learning and actions for people at all levels, to get them on board and implementing change; strategic redesign of organizational structures; and co-design of solutions by a mix of people representing a wide range of experiences of the work environment. This is what our Inclusion IMPACT® approach is.

The table below summarizes the differences between current piecemeal approaches to inclusion and our Inclusion IMPACT® approach.

Piecemeal approaches	Inclusion IMPACT®
• Are disconnected from business outcomes	• Prioritizes business outcomes
• Look for single 'silver bullet' solutions	• Addresses inclusion comprehensively: understanding, measurements, structures and actions
• Start with awareness-raising, then move on to behavior change. At some point, they may then address wider 'culture change' and systems to support it	• Starts right away with a whole system approach in which all the components in this book are indivisible and mutually reinforcing
• Assess only feelings, e.g. sense of belonging	• Assesses feelings, actions, structures and impact to identify what supports and what undermines inclusion

• Focus on developing inclusive leadership behaviors	• Shows people at all levels how to develop inclusive behavior with colleagues and stakeholders
• Struggle to engage middle managers	• Specifically involves middle managers, reveals how it benefits them and holds them accountable
• Analyze data by single identity groups, e.g. gender, ethnicity, (dis)ability	• Takes account of individuals' whole, multi-faceted identities
• Look only at people inside the organization	• Extends outward to the organization's external stakeholders for bigger, more cohesive impact
• Impose solutions based on comparison with 'best practice' in other organizations	• Co-creates tailored solutions with input from a broad mix of people connected with the organization

Envisaging an inclusive work environment

What would all this look like in practice in your organization? Based on our experience, here are some illustrations of how a genuinely inclusive work environment can operate:

- Senior leaders and managers understand and communicate the business value of being an inclusive organization

- People at all levels are rewarded for inclusive behavior that furthers organizational goals
- People are aware of each other's complementary strengths and how to combine these for the best outcomes
- Employees are skilled at enlisting different perspectives, standing in other people's shoes and questioning assumptions
- Diverse teams perform strongly because team leaders and members encourage and respect each viewpoint and work to build connection and minimize misunderstanding
- Design teams pool a broad mix of ideas from different people to co-create breakthrough products serving new or overlooked markets
- Objective, transparent and equitable processes enable the recruitment, development, engagement and retention of the most effective talent for each role and each team
- Roles are designed for people, just as services are customized for consumers
- External stakeholders, such as contractors and suppliers, hold the company in high regard because it invests in inclusive relationships with them
- Investors buy the company's shares because its 'open to all' reputation attracts strong talent and creates new markets
- There is regular measurement of progress, feedback and outcomes so that everyone can see how the organization is doing
- A broad range of individuals participate in ongoing scrutiny of the company's written and unwritten rules to build on progress and keep it open to all

- People are alive at work. Performing and climbing together, they forge deep relationships and a meaningful work environment. The organization is a crucible for powerful connections, contributions and co-creation

Which of these is happening in your organization? Congratulations if you're enabling some of them already. We'd love to hear about them. In our experience, most businesses are not yet this skilled at inclusion. Frequently there are blind spots, or unwritten rules, that stand in the way. Organizations may be doing a few things well, but missing others completely. Anything overlooked can reinforce the status quo and sabotage the organization's efforts to advance inclusion and its positive impacts.

Read on to learn how to uncover the full business potential of inclusion.

Notes

[1]   Steele, R. & Wenger, L.M. (2019). Design the Future: Breakthroughs with Diversity, Inclusion and Design Thinking. Available from https://rebekahsteele.com/design-the-future-ebook

CHAPTER 9

Bringing it to Life

Chapter 9 Sections
Uncovering the full business potential
- Why this D&I award rang hollow
- How inclusive are we?
- What's the business impact of inclusion?

Take Action: Over to you
- Actions for senior leaders, middle managers and individuals

Uncovering the full business potential

In this chapter, we use a detailed case study to show how a vast improvement in understanding and measuring inclusion yields powerful business results and clear pointers to the steps the organization needs to take.

You will find some practical actions at the end of the chapter to help you ensure that your inclusion strategy is focused on results.

Why this D&I award rang hollow

Maria*, a chief diversity and inclusion officer, was preparing for her annual presentation to the Board of Directors. Her industrial B2B company had recently won a prestigious D&I award. The CEO congratulated Maria and her team and said, "This means we're done with D&I, right?"

Maria wasn't sure how to respond. She confided to Rebekah, her executive coach, that the award felt hollow. She was not confident her organization was as inclusive as it could be. This assessment was reinforced by employee feedback. On social media, some employees were posting their surprise about the award, noting that it did not reflect their experience in the company. They questioned the award's credibility and the company's commitment to inclusion. Some had shared this feedback directly with her.

Maria, previously a head of operations, was good at producing, understanding and employing robust metrics as a basis for her business decisions. Her coach was aware of these skills and asked what metrics she was using for inclusion. Maria shared her performance scorecard (see next page), which showed in graphics how her results measured up against her projections and goals.

The first page was a summary of gender representation statistics, featuring the different percentages of women and men in leadership roles. Rebekah pointed out that these data were important, but they were actually measurements of diversity, not inclusion.

The second page of Maria's scorecard showed the percentage of favorable responses to three questions in the company's employee engagement survey, relating to inclusion at work. The third page showed how these responses varied by binary categories of sex and race. See the second and third pages below.

Inclusion Questions	% Fav	Demographic group	# of Responses	EE % Fav
I feel I am treated with respect by my manager	75%	Company overall	102,662	77%
		Sex		
I feel a sense of belonging on my team	79%	Female	22,694	70%
		Male	79,968	77%
I feel I work in an inclusive environment in which people of diverse backgrounds are valued	71%	Member of racialized group	1,690	70%
		Member of non-racialized group	100,972	75%

Second and third pages of Maria's scorecard

Rebekah asked what additional inclusion measures were being used. There weren't any.

*Name changed for anonymity

In Chapter 1, we said that inadequate understanding and measurement of inclusion was preventing business leaders answering these critically important questions:

1. How inclusive are we today?
2. What progress are we making?
3. What is leading to best results?
4. What gives us the best return on investment?
5. What should we stop doing?
6. How widespread and sustainable are the results we're seeing?
7. How is inclusion supporting our relationships with external partners?

8. How is it helping us achieve our purpose and goals?

Inadequate understanding and measurement were exactly what was happening here. As we've demonstrated, inclusion is a big concept, like sustainability. Given the pressures of business today, it is tempting to look for easy, one-off solutions, just as Maria's CEO did. They aren't going to work.

Redesigning scorecards for success. When her coach asked her the questions above, Maria could see big gaps. Her discomfort about the D&I award made sense. She really did not know how her company was performing on inclusion.

The engagement survey results indicated that 70-80% of respondents answered positively, and the company's leaders felt good about that. However, as Rebekah asked her to calculate how many individuals did not feel included, Maria realized that the remaining 20-30% amounted to between 20,000 and 30,000 people. What's more, some employees did not complete the engagement survey, and Rebekah pointed out that Maria did not know how they felt at all.

With the support of her coach, Maria woke up to the absence of real measurements for inclusion at her company.

She realized that the organization needed to address the whole of inclusion to find successful and sustainable ways to address the business challenges ahead. Benchmarking against a few engagement survey questions just wasn't providing the information the company needed.

She called on Rebekah to help her address the CEO's question in a way that would drive action, accountability and change. It was important to give the Board of Directors a vision of what was possible. Together, they began reframing his question to this:

"What measures show that an organization is being successful with inclusion?"

To design a scorecard that moved beyond a few engagement questions, Rebekah helped Maria envision an ecosystem of inclusion. The new scorecard needed to show how comprehensive investment in inclusion would impact individuals, internal and external stakeholders, and the business.

To show the board a model of how inclusive the company might be, Rebekah redesigned the scorecard, making the expanded vision clear. It comprised a set of visual summaries encapsulating insights about:

- *Who: Employees, teams, managers and senior leaders*
- *What: Feelings, actions and structures across a broad spectrum of components of inclusion*
- *Where: Internal and external*
- *When: Changes over time*
- *Why: How inclusion helps achieve critical business goals*

To bring the scorecard model to life, Rebekah included measures based on an amalgamation of real results from previous diversity and inclusion engagements with a variety of other organizations. Maria and Rebekah agreed that this would help the board envision not only what to measure, but also what possible outcomes they could aspire to achieve by advancing their own indivisible inclusion ecosystem.

How inclusive are we?

The first page of the new scorecard (see below) is designed to summarize the answer to the initial question from Chapter 1: How inclusive are we?

Graphics in the left column summarize responses to questions regarding employees' feelings about respect, authenticity and participation. It shows whether employees feel:

- Valued for their unique perspectives and talents
- Able to be their true selves at work
- Enabled to play an active part in defining the organization's purpose and how it works

How inclusive are we?

Respect

Most employees feel valued for their unique...

Perspectives   Talents

Authenticity

72%

Employees feel they can be their true self

Having a Real Say

80%

Employees feel ability to influence how this organization works is not based on status

Working *with* difference

85%

Managers know individual team members' working styles

78%

Employees are effective working with those with different working and communication styles

Openness

Most employees are consistently :

Sharing new ideas

Challenging group consensus

Challenging status quo

Speaking freely

Accountability

75%

of teams have business-linked Inclusion objectives

4 Refreshed Systems

to improve fairness & transparency: Parental leave, Succession, Innovation, Investor Relations

New Team

with multifunctional representatives to improve alignment of internal and external inclusion efforts and outcomes

Reputation   Posted on employer review website: "Inclusive workplace where all are encouraged to share ideas."

$ Selected inclusion indicators integrated into quarterly earnings press releases

First page of the new scorecard

The middle column provides insights about actions people take to work effectively with difference. This section shows whether managers are taking action to understand team members' working styles, how effective employees are at working with colleagues with different styles, and whether employees are consistently sharing new ideas, challenging consensus and speaking freely.

The right column focuses on organizational structures to enable inclusion. This section provides details on:

- Whether the performance management system requires teams to have business-linked inclusion objectives
- The policies and practices, such as parental leave, that have been reviewed and redesigned to increase inclusion
- The creation of a diverse new team tasked with aligning internal and external inclusion efforts and outcomes.

The bottom row gives insights about external reputation. It highlights a social media post by an employee about the company's inclusive working environment. It also points out that the company is addressing investors' interest in inclusion by integrating these metrics into news releases about quarterly earnings.

What's the business impact of inclusion?

Inclusive feelings, actions and structures become leading indicators of performance, innovation and bottom line achievements. The second page of the scorecard (See next page) reviews the broad impact of increased inclusion.

The top half of the second page details the potential to enhance performance when selected teams participate in a pilot applying insights from Inclusion IMPACT®. It displays performance improvements on selected measures of inclusion and related increases in business profit, patents and career growth. The bottom half of the scorecard continues the business-focused story. It highlights how pilot teams compare with control groups on measures of:

- A sense of personal responsibility for inclusion
- Manager effectiveness at driving collaborative innovation in diverse teams

Inclusive teams drive business results

After Inclusion IMPACT®, Pilot Teams reported improved levels of...

Compared to others, inclusive teams reported...

Higher sense of personal responsibility for including others
76% v. 48%

Manager effectively drives collaborative innovation
72% v. 32%

"Inclusion is about all of us and it is helping us innovate, connect to our markets, and grow our business." *Chief Innovation Officer*

Second page of the new scorecard

A quotation from an influential senior executive completes the second page of the scorecard, providing a qualitative indicator of the business value of inclusion.

How the new scorecards drove change: After reviewing the new scorecards for Maria's company, the board became committed to improving and expanding the company's inclusion strategy, how it measured inclusion, and how it demonstrated inclusion's impact on innovation and other business priorities. Rebekah followed up with development of related methods to collect and analyze the data to do so.

Take action: Over to you

These kinds of insights can help with discerning what efforts are most effective. Just as important, they can indicate practices that are not working well enough to continue and gaps that are not yet addressed. Having this information allows companies to concentrate on what generates the most valuable results.

By comparing these insights year-over-year, your company can see the progress it is making.

As we discussed in chapter 8, inclusion is not something that can be achieved and then set aside. Its dynamic nature – depending on context and experience in every moment, every interaction, every relationship – calls for comparing results in different settings and interactions as well. Consider 'experience sampling'[1]. This method to study what people feel and do during their daily work can be used to ask respondents to report on inclusion at random points over time, providing even more comprehensive metrics on which to take action.

Contrasting the original and new scorecards, which would give you the insights you need to know how you're doing with inclusion? Revisiting the questions from Chapter 1:

1. Which would give you a more complete and accurate understanding of how inclusive your company is?
2. Which would help you understand your progress and the difference it makes for your company?
3. Which would help you understand what parts of your strategy are effective?
4. Which would show where you are getting the best return on investment?
5. Which would help you understand what to *stop* doing?
6. Which contains indicators of sustainable and widespread gains in inclusiveness, such as changes to feelings, actions and organizational structures?
7. Which takes into account external stakeholders, such as contractors, investors and markets?
8. Which shows how inclusion is helping achieve the organization's business purpose and goals?

Can you now visualize the impact that a comprehensive inclusion strategy and related metrics could have on people and results in your organization?

Here are some actions to start putting this into practice.

Actions for senior leaders, middle managers and individuals

Senior Leaders

- Start putting business-linked inclusion metrics in place by embedding them into existing business scorecards. Devote part of every annual report, quarterly shareholder call, and community communication to sharing data about how your company's inclusion strategy drives better performance, decision-making, profitability and sustainability.

Middle Managers

- Add inclusion metrics to upgrade the scorecard for your part of your organization. Show how products and/or services in your remit promote inclusion (e.g. internal services such as recruitment, internal products such as business performance reports, or external products such as smart phones designed for customers with disabilities or customer support processes that can be easily tailored to different customers).

Individuals

- Suggest that your team or department begins routinely asking for feedback from others you work with closely. Seek insight about how inclusive you are and what difference that is making. Include time on team or department meeting agendas to share lessons learned and discuss opportunities for continuous improvement.

Making time: You won't have time to initiate these valuable new actions unless you eliminate something else. What can you stop doing to make room to expand inclusion?

Evaluating: Remember it's important to monitor and evaluate the impact you are making on individual, team and business success.

Addressing the big picture: Your actions are critically important to elevating inclusion. Broad organizational changes can ensure that inclusion is fully supported.

And finally … Read on for how to promote inclusion on an even bigger scale.

Notes

[1] Larson, R., & Csikszentmihalyi, M. (2014). The experience sampling method. In *Flow and the foundations of positive psychology* (pp. 21-34). Springer, Dordrecht.

"We are human only through relationship. We are really made for this delicate network of interdependence. I need you in order for me to be me – I need you to be you to the fullest. We are made for complementarity."

Archbishop Desmond Tutu,
speaking on human uniqueness and the African
spirit of Ubuntu, 2013[1]

CHAPTER 10

A Greater Whole

Chapter 10 Sections

Raising ambitions for prosperity and progress

HAVING READ THIS FAR, you will be clear why we need to radically rethink inclusion in the way we've proposed in this book.

You may already have had this vision for your organization. You may have seen tensions undermining your own work environment or your relationships with external partners: talent being wasted, energy sapped, or business opportunities missed because they do not fit 'the norm'. You may have wished something could be done. Now there is a practical way forward to make the progress you long for and achieve your organization's purpose.

For many, that will be reason enough to take action now.

When you commit to a comprehensive strategy for inclusion, you are starting to build healthier, more purposeful and sustainable organizations that benefit by harnessing the power of everyone.

Yet there is even more to it than that.

Leaders who are truly ambitious for inclusion recognize that organizations are part of a greater whole. We explained in Chapter 7 why you cannot be fully successful with inclusion inside your organization unless you take account of the wider system in which you operate. If this wider system perpetuates exclusion and inequality, it will remain a struggle to get the results you need from inclusion internally.

To change the wider system in favor of inclusion requires collective action. We can start by challenging how our societies think about, organize and measure human progress.

Just as many companies have found measuring inclusion difficult, governments have struggled to measure human prosperity and wellbeing in anything other than hard economic data. There is pressure for that to change.

Measuring inclusion across society

Interest is growing in the idea that economic progress cannot, and should not, be measured by money alone. More income makes people happy, but only up to a point, as

Dame Minouche Shafik, director of the London School of Economics and Political Science, explained at the 2019 Davos summit.

"Everything is not about GDP and can't be measured in units of money," she said. "Having good health – both physical and mental health – good relationships, and meaningful work … are the key drivers of what makes people happy. Those are important things that economists should increasingly measure."[2]

Inclusion enhances those essentials, while exclusion puts them at risk. A group of forward-thinking leaders from around the world were invited to craft ambitious solutions at a Diversity, Equity and Inclusion Futures Event in the US.[3] During an open space forum at the start, participants were invited to 'stand in the future' and ask game-changing questions to determine the agenda for the event. Rebekah asked: "What if GWI (Gross World Inclusion) replaced GDP (Gross Domestic Product)?"

The ripple of exclamations around the room signaled the resonance of the idea. Prioritizing the topic, participants explored what changes would be required to realize this vision. What would it mean to create key performance indicators measuring our connectedness with our fellow humans and with the natural world on which our continued existence depends?

GDP data focus on the outcomes of single-minded competition for finite materials and financial growth. GWI would enable understanding of what's happening in global and local communities to advance human capabilities and human rights, the sharing and preservation of natural resources and the opportunity for all individuals to have a voice.

Those engaged in this mental exercise recognized that GDP measures are not going to go away. Nor did they advocate for that. But they saw how GWI expands our thinking, by looking beyond the monetary value of economic prosperity and progress.

If organizations, large and small, collectively sought to perform better on measures of inclusion, as well as financial measures, they would discover the interplay between these factors. They could challenge themselves to build a robust economy powered by the value created by unlocking every person's wellbeing and potential.

Collective action for inclusion

We already see some signs of this happening.

Just as leading companies have joined forces to prioritize sustainability across their operations and advocate for action on the climate emergency, there are now organizations that are collectively addressing inclusion as an issue of global importance for prosperity and progress.

The following initiatives, while specifically focused on gender, give pointers to what could be achieved by collaborative efforts to promote inclusion even more broadly across society:

The Unstereotype Alliance: This industry-led initiative was convened by UN Women in 2017 to tackle harmful gender stereotypes and use the power of advertising to shape realistic, non-biased perceptions of women and men. The vice-chairs are Interpublic Group, Safaricom Twaweza, and Unilever. Members include giant corporations such as Alibaba, Diageo, Google, P&G, Vodafone and WPP.[4]

These big brands and advertising companies have signed up to a code of principles which include depicting people as empowered actors, portraying multidimensional personalities and refraining from objectifying people. They have committed to challenging each other as advertisers and agencies to create and buy only the best 'unstereotyped' marketing and advertising content.

As well as producing guidelines for companies to follow, their collective authority has been used to condemn and remove advertising that trivializes violence against women, such as an online cartoon of a man punching a woman for not buying the brand of burger he wanted.[5]

Male Champions of Change Global Technology Group: The tech sector is shaping and influencing the future of the human race in dramatic ways. Yet it risks being held back and making mistakes because of the lack of diversity in its leadership and workforce. In early 2019, a coalition of tech CEOs wrote an open letter, published in the Financial Times, calling on male tech leaders to take responsibility for accelerating gender equality and to commit to "listen, learn, and lead through action".

The coalition, working with accelerateHER, which campaigns to break down barriers to women in technology, advocates a strategy of systemic change. It has identified 10 areas of action both inside and outside organizations, which include closing the gender pay gap, making all roles flexible, avoiding the 'merit' trap, tackling everyday sexism in society and taking action against domestic violence.[6]

Sustainability and inclusion are interdependent

Growing attention is being paid to the common ground between broad inclusion and sustainability, as we noted in Chapter 1. The research and design we have done for this book have led us see inclusion and sustainability as interdependent. Both require global systemic change. Both also require shifts in behavior, towards our fellow humans and towards preservation of our natural environment.

We see this interdependence emerging at different levels of organizations and society.

Grassroots level: Bjørn Z. Ekelund, an expert in collaboration across style differences, has worked with multiple culturally diverse populations on finding solutions for environmental sustainability. He has found that a deliberately inclusive process can speed up grassroots behavior change to tackle the climate crisis.

"For this cross-cultural work, you have to create an atmosphere of psychological safety and trust where people feel able to share their perspectives and where they really listen to each other," he says. "With an intentionally inclusive process, people generate more innovative solutions, make higher quality decisions, take charge and feel ownership. No time is wasted between defining solutions and implementing them. This is very different from the time it can take to implement top-down solutions."[7]

Organizational level: Corporate responsibility, inclusion and diversity can all provide purpose, build trust, and drive innovation, according to Common Purpose, a report published by Sodexo on the intersection of the two corporate functions in the U.S. Currently, they often compete for scarce resources and do not embrace each other's mission. The report calls on them to align and collaborate, saying "This could mark the next logical stage of evolution for D&I and CR, a new phase that leads to even greater value for shareholders, customers, employees and other stakeholders."[8]

Cross-industry level: There is a collection of organizations known as B Corps that is committed to using business as a force for good. Individually, certified B Corp companies demonstrate positive social and environmental impact. Collectively, they aim for a global economy that is focused on the long term, works for everyone and protects the natural environment on which our future depends.

Until recently, however, the B Corp movement has not paid enough attention to diversity, equity and inclusion (DEI), says Ryan Honeyman, co-author of *The B Corp Handbook*, now in its second edition.

Honeyman says that in recent years he has realized that "there is no such thing as a conversation about DEI and a separate conversation about business as a force for good. They are the same conversation. Siloing DEI into something separate is one of the main barriers facing our movement to create a more equitable society."[9]

Given these overlapping goals, we envisage a new category – an 'IN Corps' of organizations ambitiously focused on inclusion – joining forces with B Corp organizations to create a bigger and more impactful movement for change. We believe that what we have proposed in this book – a comprehensive way to understand, measure and act on inclusion – would powerfully complement the stringent standards required to achieve and maintain B Corp status.

We expect to see more companies setting the pace with strategies built on the interdependent goals of inclusion and sustainability and acting in concert with others to effect wider change more quickly. Combining inclusion and sustainability in the different ways we have described above would bring fresh perspectives that increase the likelihood of finding breakthrough solutions to our most pressing challenges, most notably the climate emergency.

The indivisible whole

In this book, we have challenged the limitations of prevailing approaches to inclusion and proposed a far more ambitious, holistic alternative.

Organizations that place inclusion at the heart of their business strategy will be better equipped to thrive in the fast changing world of work. They will create stronger links with workers, customers, suppliers, investors, regulators and other stakeholders. They will act to influence the wider system around them and enhance their own efforts by learning from the best in other parts of the economy. They will tie all of this to business performance and sustainability, in an indivisible whole.

This work, like any business initiative to improve results and impact, takes investment, time and hard work. It involves radically rethinking how to achieve impact. It also requires determination to succeed.

To make the most of the valuable differences that each person brings, we must constantly challenge our own assumptions and prejudices. The African spirit of Ubuntu, as explained by Archbishop Desmond Tutu, is about human interconnectedness. People with Ubuntu have the self-assurance of knowing that they belong to 'a greater whole' and that they are diminished when others are treated as if they were less than who they are.

It is possible to shift away from fear and mistrust towards openness and caring about the perspectives of everybody. It is possible to take responsibility to make inclusion happen, in ourselves, in our teams, in our organizations and in our world. All of this is possible when we see our indivisible humanity.

Notes

[1] Tutu, D. (2013). Archbishop Desmond Tutu, speaking as 2013 Templeton Prize laureate on Who we are: Human uniqueness and the African spirit of Ubuntu. Retrieved from https://www.youtube.com/watch?v=0wZtfqZ271w

[2] Shafik, M. (2019). Dame Minouche Shafik, speaking at WEF 2019. Retrieved from https://youtu.be/3D5_H0aG12A

[3] DEI Futures Event. (2018, April). Organized by Julie O'Mara and colleagues in Princeton, New Jersey

[4] #Unstereotype Alliance: https://www.unstereotypealliance.org/en

[5] The Unstereotype Alliance. (2019, October 11). Unstereotype Alliance statement regarding the #BickyBurger advert. Retrieved from: https://www.unstereotypealliance.org/en/news-and--events/press-releases/oct-11-2019. See also: BBC News (2019, October 10). Bicky Burger removes 'sickening, irresponsible' Facebook advert. Retrieved from www.bbc.co.uk/news/world-europe-49998664

[6] MCC Global Technology Group. (2019, January 25). Open letter to Technology Industry Leaders in Financial Times. Available from https://malechampionsofchange.com/mcc-global-technology-group-open-letter-to-technology-industry

[7] Interview with authors (2020, February). Ekelund is author of several books including *Unleashing the Power of Diversity: How to open minds for good*

[8] Anand, R., Sylvan, R. & Lilani, R. (2019). *Common Purpose, The intersection of Diversity & Inclusion and Corporate Responsibility in the United States*. Retrieved from https://us.sodexo.com/files/live/sites/com-us/files/our-impact/Common-PurposePaperFINAL.pdf

[9] Honeyman, R. (2019, April 4). We Need to Talk: Why B Corps Need to Get Serious about Diversity, Equity, & Inclusion. Retrieved from https://ideas.bkconnection.com/we-need-to-talk-why-b-corps-need-to-get-serious-about-diversity-equity-inclusion

AFTERWORD

An Invitation

We hope this book has inspired you. If you would like to know more, or would welcome help in implementing the strategies and actions we propose, we invite you to get in touch.

We also know that there are some organizations that are already making great strides with inclusion. We would welcome connecting with you so we can learn from each other and share each other's stories more widely.

We are enthusiastic about blazing this trail together with people who share our vision.

Whether you are just starting out, or reconsidering your strategy in order to make greater progress, or at the leading edge of next-level inclusion and sustainability, you can contact us this way:

Alison at www.alisonmaitland.com/contact

Rebekah at https://rebekahsteele.com/contactme

We look forward to hearing from you!

Appendices

Appendix 1: Summary of Actions with Chapter number

Chapter 2

Senior Leaders
- Start to ask this question in every strategy meeting: "Who will share a different idea to help us be more discerning and more creative?"
- Explore with colleagues how you can formalize this as part of every business meeting in your organization.

Middle Managers
- Ask your direct reports what you can do to make it easy for each of them to speak freely and share their ideas and dissenting opinions.
- Use their guidance to adjust how you run meetings.
- Share what you learn with other managers.

Individuals

- Help others on your team to speak up by making opportunities to listen, ask questions, and create a safe space.
- Talk with your co-workers and manager about how to ensure that everyone has a voice, including in how the team operates and how work gets done.

Chapter 3

Senior Leaders

- Collaborate with middle managers to establish clear expectations about their inclusion performance and results.
- Discuss how these will help them achieve their objectives, and improve their relationships with employees and stakeholders.
- Support their success by weaving expectations into talent processes such as performance management, succession and rewards.

Middle Managers

- Start an informal coaching group with a mix of junior and senior colleagues at different levels and in different parts of the organization.
- Focus on feedback, sharing ideas, and encouraging each other to succeed.
- Make time to co-create ways to support each other's commitment to inclusion, and start practicing these every day.

Individuals

- Check in regularly with your colleagues to make sure they feel supported and involved with how things are going in the team, on your joint project, or in the organization generally.

- You can set the example, even if you're not the team leader. Encourage your manager to establish a process enabling this for teams across the organization.

Chapter 4

Senior Leaders

- Take time to reflect on what your organization is missing if it focuses only on feelings of inclusion.
- Initiate a formal and transparent assessment of how inclusive behaviors are at every level of the company, and what formal structures are in place.
- Make space and time to discuss with your colleagues what hidden assumptions you may be making that hinder a diverse mix of talent from progressing in the organization.

Middle Managers

- Establish a commitment to transparency in your team. Talk about how decisions are made about people and their opportunities and rewards at work.
- Ask for suggestions about how the formal processes and informal expectations that impact those decisions could be amended to yield fairer outcomes. Implement changes.
- Signal clearly that you believe everyone in your team has the potential to succeed.

Individuals

- Consider how common modes of operating (e.g. an expectation to work long hours) within your team might be limiting fairness.

- Explore these dynamics with your manager and colleagues to create change together. Avoid blaming. Focus on the opportunity to create more just processes that help the organization achieve its goals.
- Decide on ways to have these kinds of discussions regularly.

Chapter 5

Senior Leaders

- When making choices that affect workers, consistently ask if all are included, if all will benefit (and no one will be harmed). Ask "Who have we inadvertently left out?"
- What adjustments can you make to give employees greater autonomy and choice?
- Carve out time to work with other leaders to integrate these criteria formally into all decision making.

Middle Managers

- Ask your team to share how each of them prefers to work (e.g. morning/evening person; solo/collaborator; quiet/stimulating environment; preliminary chit-chat/straight to the point).
- Make time to discuss how you can adjust meetings and working relationships to take these different preferences into account to accomplish shared goals more effectively. How can you cater to each worker in personalized ways when feasible?

Individuals

- Next time you are part of a joint project, start by asking your colleagues how they work best and inform them of your own preferences.
- Share your learning from this experience with your manager and broader team.

- Drawing on this knowledge, co-create ways to improve the efficiency of joint projects.

Chapter 6

Senior Leaders

- Begin a reciprocal mentorship with someone who is different from you, with a focus on helping each other become more inclusive leaders.
- Use the 10 enablers as discussion points for that development work. Consider what you can learn from this process that would be useful to incorporate as a standard part of leadership development.

Middle Managers

- Formally commit to working on all three sets of inclusion enablers – connection, opportunity, and common cause – to increase team collaboration in achieving a critical performance objective.
- Discuss how to do this with your team, work on it with a peer coaching group, and/or find someone with insight and expertise to guide you.

Individuals

- Partner with colleagues to explore which of the 10 enablers are strengths that you already consistently weave into your collective work.
- Work together on a plan to address gaps individually and as a team. Share your plan with others, and invite colleagues from other parts of the organization to join in.

Chapter 7

Senior Leaders

- Start a conversation with your board of directors about seizing opportunities to promote inclusion by addressing external stakeholders' needs. Focus on ways to do this that will have a positive impact on employee experience, team performance, product and service design, and/or reputation.
- Add progress on inclusion into your discussions with investors about Environmental, Social and Governance issues.

Middle Managers

- Actively seek input from customers about their unmet needs and potential solutions (products or services) that you can create together. Do the same with contractors and suppliers. Use this information to update and customize your inclusion processes for greater impact.
- Find ways to share joint progress that enhance your company's reputation with these stakeholders.

Individuals

- Ask your manager to devote part of each team meeting to gathering input for big upcoming decisions, so you have an active part in defining how the organization works.
- Run a session with colleagues, including support staff, where everyone shares a 'hidden talent' (e.g. speaking an additional language). Discuss how the team can use these to achieve common goals.

Chapter 9

Senior Leaders

- Start putting business-linked inclusion metrics in place by embedding them into existing business scorecards. Devote part of every annual report, quarterly shareholder call, and community communication to sharing data about how your company's inclusion strategy drives better performance, decision-making, profitability and sustainability.

Middle Managers

- Add inclusion metrics to upgrade the scorecard for your part of your organization. Show how products and/or services in your remit promote inclusion (e.g. internal services such as recruitment, internal products such as business performance reports, or external products such as smart phones designed for customers with disabilities or customer support processes that can be easily tailored to different customers).

Individuals

- Suggest that your team or department begins routinely asking for feedback from others you work with closely. Seek insight about how inclusive you are and what difference that is making. Include time on team or department meeting agendas to share lessons learned and discuss opportunities for continuous improvement.

Making Time: Taking action means starting new habits. To be successful, you also need to consider what you will *stop* doing. Rather than hoping to find time for inclusion, intentionally structure in time to connect with people, to listen to someone with whom you disagree, to implement the suggestions in this book and to develop the capabilities to do this well.

Meanwhile, put an end to old routines that work against your inclusion efforts. For example, you might stop 'multitasking' on your smartphone in meetings instead of giving all colleagues your full attention. Or stop using idioms and metaphors that are specific to one culture. Or stop assuming that colleagues who rarely speak up in meetings have nothing to say and instead intentionally invite their contribution. Eliminate time-wasting diversions in order to open up the time you need to begin your new steps to build inclusion.

Evaluating: Monitor and evaluate the impact you make with these actions on individual engagement, team performance, and business success. You can do this formally if you're a senior leader or middle manager, or informally if you are an individual contributor.

Addressing the big picture: Remember that your organization must complement individual action with systemic changes across the organization.

Appendix 2: Diagram of the 5Ws of Inclusion IMPACT®

The INdivisible Whole

Individual, Business and
Social Impact

Demonstrated
over time

Feelings   Actions   Structures

Individuals

Connection
• Openness
• Respect
• Trust

Teams

Inclusion
Enablers

Managers

Opportunity   Common Cause
• Fairness   • Shared power
• Transparency   • Participation
• Choice   • Support
                        • Shared purpose

Senior Leaders

With internal and
external stakeholders

The components of the INdivisible Whole

Who

Individuals

Teams

Managers

Senior Leaders

What

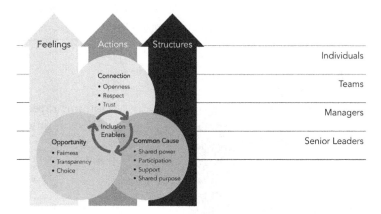

Where

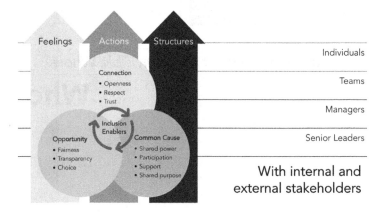

With internal and external stakeholders

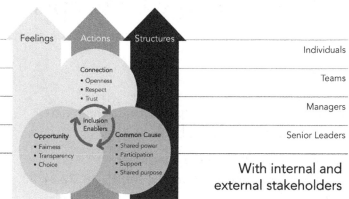

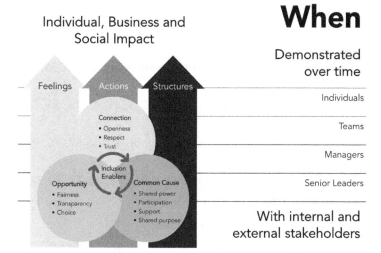

Index of Key Concepts

This index is designed to guide you to the main concepts and ideas in the book.

Inclusion is also important for social and environmental sustainability

To achieve desired outcomes, organizations need to radically rethink inclusion

To have impact, inclusion requires a whole-system approach (**the 5 Ws, Inclusion IMPACT®**)

About the authors

Alison Maitland is a writer, speaker, adviser and coach. She is co-author of two previous books, *Future Work* and *Why Women Mean Business*. A former long-serving journalist with the *Financial Times*, she is a Senior Fellow in Human Capital at The Conference Board and a Senior Visiting Fellow at Cass Business School, London. She is Chair of the Cass Global Women's Leadership Programme Executive Board and has served as Vice Chair of the International Women's Forum UK. She was Director of The Conference Board's European Council for Diversity and Inclusion in Business for nine years. **www.alisonmaitland.com**

Rebekah Steele is a business strategist, innovator and speaker with deep expertise in Diversity and Inclusion. Building on two decades in the corporate world, including as a senior leader in Fortune 500 companies, Rebekah launched her consultancy focused on the intersection of diversity, inclusion and human-centered design thinking. She helps leaders in business, government and non-profit organizations bring progressive strategies to life via her signature D&I innovation labs and distinctive ecosystem design process. Canada-based and globally engaged, Rebekah speaks widely on next generation D&I and is also a Senior Fellow and Council Director with The Conference Board. **rebekahsteele.com**

About the illustrator

J. Rodes Gardner is an American artist and illustrator born and raised in Richmond, Virginia. Capable with a range of styles and media, he is particularly drawn to fantastical images in pencil or ink. While drawing is a favored pursuit of his, he aspires to be a 'Renaissance Man' as he is fascinated by a wide array of disciplines including visual arts, music and medical science. He earned his bachelor's degree in Biological Science with University Honors at the University of Mary Washington. While there, he conducted a study on the relative value of palatable food versus social play in young rats. Resonating with themes in *INdivisible* addressing the human need for inclusion, the study's results indicated that social and physical interactions may rightly be considered a necessity in young mammals.

Made in the USA
Monee, IL
09 December 2020